PLEASING GOD

PLEASING
GOD
RC SPROUL

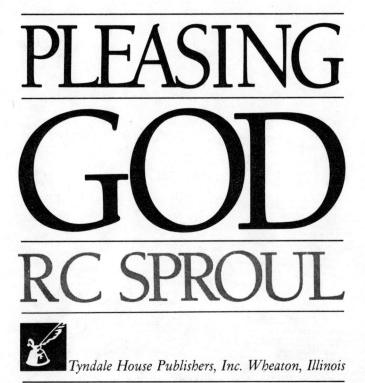

Tyndale House Publishers, Inc. Wheaton, Illinois

Scripture quotations, unless otherwise indicated,
are from *The Holy Bible, New King James Version,*
copyright 1982 by Thomas Nelson, Inc.

Scripture quotations marked NASB are from *New
American Standard Bible,* copyright 1960, 1962,
1963, 1971, 1973 by The Lockman Foundation.

First printing, May 1988

Library of Congress Catalog Card Number
88-50173

ISBN 0-8423-4968-5, cloth

Copyright 1988 by R. C. Sproul

Printed in the United States of America

For Chuck and Pam Green
and
Dale and Joyce Linder,
People who love to please God

C O N T E N T S

PREFACE

"This is My beloved Son, in whom I am well pleased" (Matt. 3:17).

There are three occasions in the New Testament when God speaks audibly from heaven: Jesus' baptism (Matt. 3:17; Mark 1:11; Luke 3:22), the Transfiguration (Matt. 17:5; Mark 9:7; Luke 9:35), and Jesus' address after the triumphal entry (John 12:28). On the first two of these occasions God declares that He is pleased with His Son. What higher approval could a man enjoy than to know that what he has done is pleasing to God? Every Christian should have a passion to please God. We are to delight in honoring Him. It is our own greatest pleasure to please our Redeemer. We all begin the Christian life with the intention of living in such a way as to please God. But we encounter obstacles along the way. We meet with conflicts between what pleases us and what pleases God.

We need help in overcoming these obstacles. In a real way the Christian life is often a struggle. We gain ground and then slip backwards. There is such a thing as backsliding. Sometimes the slide seems as if it is greased with the slickest substance the Devil can use. But as children who totter at the top of a sliding board, fearful to move, we have a heavenly Father who guards the edge of the board and who waits at the bottom of the slide to catch us in His arms.

This book is intended as a practical guide for Christian living. It is not a weighty scholarly volume. It is an attempt to provide help for the struggle in which we are involved.

The book was suggested by my editor, Dr. Wendell Hawley, who has a profound concern for helping Christians who are struggling to please God.

Special thanks for this book go to Dr. Hawley and to my secretary, Mrs. Maureen Buchman, who assisted in its preparation. Again, special thanks to my most ruthless editor, my wife, Vesta, who wields a cruel red pen.

Orlando 1987

CHAPTER ONE
TENDER GRACE

"I see men like trees, walking" (Mark 8:24). What a strange experience. Walking trees are not a normal sight for normal people. But the man who saw "walking trees" was a man in transition. He was at an intermediate stage between total blindness and full clarity of vision. He was, as we shall see, a representative of all Christians in their progress toward pleasing God.

When the Bible records the miracle healings wrought by Jesus, the healings are usually instantaneous and complete. Jesus did not partially raise Lazarus from the dead. The man with the withered arm did not recover in stages. In most other miracles, the person was changed instantly.

So the episode recorded in Mark's Gospel is unusual. It records the healing of a blind man in two stages:

And they came to Bethsaida. And they brought a blind man to Him, and entreated Him to touch him. And taking the blind man by the hand, He brought him out of the village; and after spitting on his eyes, and laying His hands upon him, He asked him, "Do you see anything?" And he looked up and said, "I see men, for I am seeing them like trees, walking about." Then again He laid His hands upon his eyes; and he looked intently and was restored, and began to see everything clearly.
Mark 8:22-25, NASB

This is a story of the power and the grace of Christ. It is a story of *tender grace*. When Jesus was approached by people concerned about the plight of the blind man, the first act He performed was to "take the blind man by the hand." Holding his hand, Jesus led the man out of town.

Picture the scene. The Son of God surely had the power to heal the man on the spot. Instead, Jesus led him away from the crowd. He ministered to him in private. The blind man was not a spectacle for the curious to gaze upon. Our Lord directed the man's steps. Never in his life did the blind man have so secure a guide. There was no danger of falling, no menace of tripping. He was being led by the hand of Christ.

Had Jesus' act of tenderness ended at that point, I'm sure it would have been enough. The blind man could tell the story to his life's end. "He touched me!" he could exclaim, and he would have savored the experience forever. But Jesus was not finished. He took the next step.

When they were away from the crowd Jesus did something that could offend our sensibilities. He spit on the man's eyes. Now, to have someone spit in our eye is to experience a shameful, degrading insult. But the purpose of Jesus was not to insult, but to heal. He touched the man and asked him if he could see anything.

It was at this point that the man began to see men as walking trees. He saw what any blind man would give anything to see. His vision was dim, blurred—but he could see. Moments earlier he could see nothing. His eyes were useless. He lived in perpetual darkness. But now, suddenly, he could discern moving forms. He could detect the difference between light and shadow. A new world was opening before him. No longer would he require that someone lead him by the hand. He could throw away his cane.

Jesus was not finished. He applied a second touch. With the second touch the things that were blurred came into sharp focus. Now the man could clearly distinguish between trees and men. Now he saw trees standing still, their branches swaying gently in the breeze. He saw men as men, walking. He could discern the difference between short men and tall men, fat men and thin men, young men and old men. He was beginning to recognize the minute facial characteristics that provoke recognition of distinctive personal identities. Perhaps he could have done it before by means of touch. Possibly he could have run his fingers over a person's face and recognized certain people. He surely would not have noticed the unique sounds of different people's voices. But now he could keep his hands in his pockets and still know who was standing before him. The first face he saw clearly was the face of Christ. For him it was the beginning of the blessed vision.

Though the Bible doesn't say so, it appears certain that his eyes were not the only part of the man that was healed. With the touch of Christ comes also the healing of the heart. His heart of stone had been changed to a heart of flesh, pulsating anew with spiritual life.

The story of this healing was not intended as just a parable of the Christian's spiritual renewal. The event was a real miracle in space and time, a prodigious display of the power of Christ. But it serves us well as a parallel of spiritual renewal.

The Bible uses the metaphor of blindness to describe

our fallen estate. We are all men born blind. We enter this world in a state of spiritual darkness. We do not see the things of the kingdom of God. By nature we have scales upon our eyes, cataracts so thick that we cannot even perceive men as trees, walking. It requires a special act of tender grace for us to see the kingdom of God.

THE BEGINNING: REGENERATION

The act of grace by which our eyes are opened to the things of God is *regeneration*, spiritual rebirth. It is an act that only God can perform. We are no more able to regenerate ourselves than a blind man is able to see by a sheer act of the will. A blind man can decide to see, but he cannot see unless his eyes are healed.

Regeneration does not take place in stages. It is instantaneous. It is accomplished by one touch of the Holy Spirit upon our souls. It is a sovereign work, a thoroughly effective work accomplished by the immediate power of the omnipotence of God. Only God can bring something out of nothing and life out of death. Only God can quicken the human soul.

When God quickens a human soul He does it *immediately*. When I say "immediately" I do not mean immediate with respect to time, though indeed it happens spontaneously. I mean by the term that He does it directly without *means*, without the use of secondary causes. (The Latin word *immediatus* actually meant "without intermediary.")

When I am sick I do two things. I pray and I take my medicine. I ask that God will bring healing to me by means of the medicine. I ask God to guide the doctor's hands, to guide the means of healing by His special providence.

Yet when Jesus healed the blind man, He did not use any indirect means. No medicine was necessary. Jesus could heal by the sound of His voice. I am puzzled by the narrative at one point. Why did Jesus spit upon the man's eyes? Why did He have the leper bathe in the pool of Siloam? Obviously the power was not in the spit or in the water of the pool. On other occasions Jesus dispensed with such devices. His power was direct and immediate.

So it is with our regeneration. We are required to be bathed with the water of baptism. But the water in the baptismal pool does not contain a magic elixir to redeem human souls. The water is a sign that points beyond itself to the living water that makes us alive. It is an outward, concrete symbol of the healing power of God.

There is another parallel, however, in the story of the healing of the blind man. Though we are regenerated instantly by the sovereign power of God and are transferred immediately from the kingdom of darkness into the kingdom of light, our sanctification is indeed in stages.

When we are born again we see men as trees, walking. Our spiritual vision is clouded. We do not see all things in sharp spiritual focus. Our vision is still clouded by ongoing sin. There will come a day when all remnants of our old nature will be destroyed. There will come a day when our hearts will be so purified that Christ's beatitude will be fulfilled: "Blessed are the pure in heart, for they shall see God" (Matthew 5:8). This is what many Christians in the Middle Ages called the "beatific vision."

The work of perfecting our spiritual state is called *glorification*. Glorification does not take place in this life. We must wait for heaven for our sanctification to be complete. Now, though we see what we could not see before, we still see through a glass darkly.

In this life we need the second touch of Christ. Indeed we require a third, fourth, fifth, and continual touch. Though the scales are removed from our eyes, we still need to be led by the hand of Jesus.

Regeneration is the beginning of a journey. It is a journey with successes and failures, with growth amidst stumbling. At times the progress seems painfully slow, but progress is there. It is a movement to sharper focus—a life that begins with a touch of tender grace that moves toward more grace.

Sisyphus was the tragic hero of an ancient Greek myth. Because he had offended the gods he was doomed to an everlasting hell of repeated and constant frustration. His task was to push a huge boulder up a steep hill. It took all of his strength to move the rock.

Every time he reached the top, the boulder rolled over and crashed once more to the bottom. Sisyphus' task required that he race to the bottom to start all over again. His task was never finished. No final progress was achieved.

Sometimes Christians feel like Sisyphus. Progress seems so slow in the Christian life that it feels like we are walking in place, spinning our wheels, doubling our efforts and gaining no ground.

The image that captures the torture of the damned is the image of the circle. The circle goes round and round with no beginning and no end—merely endless repetition.

Consider the punishment of Samson. After he revealed the secret of his strength to his traitorous lover, Delilah, he was captured by the Philistines. His dreadful disgrace is summarized by one verse in the Bible:

Then the Philistines seized him and gouged out his eyes; and they brought him down to Gaza and bound him with bronze chains, and he was a grinder in the prison.
Judges 16:21, NASB

I don't really know what a grinder in a Philistine prison did. I do remember how the job was depicted by Hollywood. I have vague memories of an old film about Samson. Victor Mature played the mighty man of Israel. The scene that sticks in my mind is that of the blinded Samson replacing an ox on the wheel of a grinding machine. The ox was yoked to a lever that turned the gears of the machine as the ox plodded around in a circle, wearing a rut in the ground. I can see Victor Mature with vacant eyes, his muscles glistening with sweat, walking around and around in an endless cycle of toil, getting nowhere, only digging the rut of his path deeper and deeper.

That is the brutal image of the circle.

THE CONTINUATION: SANCTIFICATION

But the Christian life is not futile like that. It does not follow the pattern of the circle. The image of the Christian life is a line. It has a beginning, a middle, and an end. There is an end goal of glory. The God who started all things in the beginning has a goal for His people. We reach ahead for the day when we hear Christ say, "Come, my beloved, enter the kingdom which my Father has prepared for you."

With the apostle Paul we say, "Forgetting what lies behind and reaching forward to what lies ahead, I press on toward the goal for the prize of the upward call of God in Christ Jesus" (Philippians 3:13, NASB). In the Christian life there is an *upward call*. One does not move upward in a circle. We are on a line that is going somewhere. It is moving forward. In a word, there is *progress* to the Christian life.

We remember the classic of Christian literature written by John Bunyan, *The Pilgrim's Progress*. The pilgrim is the Christian who moves toward heaven. His progress is made slow and cumbersome by the weight he carries on his back. He faces obstacles at every turn. He is threatened by the Slough of Despond. He is tripped up by the likes of Mr. Worldlywise.

Bunyan understood the many temptations and pitfalls that stand in the path of every Christian. But he also understood two vitally important truths about the Christian life: We are pilgrims, and we make progress.

A pilgrim is one who is on a journey. His travels take him to strange places. He is a person on the move. Like the Old Testament Hebrew, a Christian pilgrim lives in tents. He is a seminomad. He is never so at home in this world that he completely settles in. Life is always a frontier for him. The water he drinks is never stagnant. Like Abraham, the father of the faithful, he searches for a better country whose builder and maker is God. All of God's people are pilgrims and sojourners on the earth.

All Christians make progress. Progress is made certain by the indwelling Holy Spirit who refuses to allow us to stand still. Oh, we try to stand still. We even regress. Like the disciples, we hide in our upper rooms, huddled in fear. But Jesus will not allow us to stay there.

No one is born a Christian. By nature we are flesh. The Christian life begins with the work of the Holy Spirit in rebirth. The term "born-again Christian" is almost a misnomer. It is a redundancy. It is a kind of theological stuttering. If one is born again, then he is a Christian. If he is a Christian, than he is born again. There are no nonborn-again Christians and no born-again non-Christians. To be reborn is to be born into Christ by the Holy Spirit. This is a prerequisite for the Christian life. It is also the genesis, the beginning of the Christian life.

Everyone starts the Christian life the same way: We all start by being born again. Our experiences of rebirth may differ, but the fact of rebirth is necessary for all of us.

It is important for us to understand that no two Christians begin their Christian walk with the same baggage. Some people are born again at five years old, some at fifty-five. Some come to faith from a well-disciplined background, others from a life of riotous and unbridled

21

wildness. We struggle with different sins. We carry mixed and matched luggage.

Some of us know the day and the hour we were converted. Others have no distinct recollection of when we were reborn. Billy Graham speaks of a meeting held by Mordecai Ham where he met Christ. Ruth Graham can't pinpoint within five years the date of her conversion. Some people weep at conversion, others are giddy with joy.

It is a grave mistake to insist that everybody display the same outward signs of conversion that we experienced. Those with a sudden and dramatic conversion experience tend to be suspicious of those who cannot name the day and the hour. Those whose experience is less dramatic may wonder about the emotional stability of those who cite a sudden experience.

Here we must honor the work of the Holy Spirit, who convicts people in different ways at different times. The ultimate question we face is not *when* we were converted or *where* we were converted. The only real question is whether we *are* converted. If we are born of the Spirit, then we are brothers and sisters to all who are in Christ.

Paul tells us:

For by grace you have been saved through faith; and that not of yourselves, it is the gift of God; not as a result of works, that no one should boast. For we are His workmanship, created in Christ Jesus for good works, which God prepared beforehand that we should walk in them. Ephesians 2:8-10, NASB

At this point we are all equal. None of us has converted ourselves. Rebirth is the work of God. We are the workmanship or the craftsmanship of Christ. Christ is the master craftsman. His workmanship is neither dull nor monotonous. When He redeems us He does not destroy our identity nor our individuality. Each Christian is a distinctive work of art fashioned by Christ. Each redeemed person is literally a masterpiece.

Jesus does not fashion His art on an assembly line. His work of molding and shaping is done with infinite care and patience. We've seen the bumper sticker that reads, "Please be patient with me; God is not finished with me yet."

Sanctification is a process. It is a gradual process. Run for your life from those who promise you instant sanctification. There is a poisonous doctrine—one that dies hard in Christian circles—called the doctrine of perfectionism. It teaches that some people have already attained spiritual perfection in this world. They promise a "second work of grace," a "second blessing" of instant sanctification. From such teachers turn away.

I was a Christian for only a few months when I met my first preacher of instant sanctification. He offered to lay hands on me and pray that I receive the second blessing. I found the idea very attractive. The most serious frustration I experienced in my new Christian life was that I was still sinning. I had experienced profound victory in some parts of my life, but other areas seemed very stubborn. I was already acutely aware of the ongoing warfare between the flesh and the Spirit.

I prayed with the preacher for instant sanctification. It didn't work. The second blessing eluded me. Martin Luther, who spent so much of his early life trying to be completely righteous, had said, "If ever a man could get to heaven through monkery [faithfully living the monastic life], it was I." I was thinking that if ever a man could get the second blessing by seeking it, it was I.

The preacher was convinced that my sin was blocking my efforts to gain release from my sin. I was caught in the most vicious of circles. What the minister was actually saying to me was that if I was going to get rid of my sin I had to first get rid of my sin. In other words, all I needed before I could get the second blessing was the second blessing.

Finally, another minister helped me out of this hopeless dilemma. I soon realized that the idea of a second blessing that would give me instant sanctification was a pious fraud.

Since that experience I have met two people who claimed they had attained perfect sanctification. Their Christian lives were tragic. For people to convince themselves that they have already achieved spiritual perfection, they must do one or both of two things: They must so reduce the demands of God's law to such a low level that they can obey them, or they must radically inflate their own assessment of their spiritual performance.

Either of these steps is deadly. To reduce the demands of God's law is to do violence against the holiness of God. To inflate one's own self-assessment to the point of self-delusion is an extreme form of pride.

Sanctification requires far more than a quick experience of the laying on of hands. Rebirth is instantaneous. Justification is instantaneous. *But sanctification is a lifelong process.* It involves a diligent struggle against a multitude of obstacles. It is like the journey of Bunyan's pilgrim, filled with pitfalls and laden with perils. It is a journey that takes us through the dark night of the soul, through the valley of the shadow of death, and through the wilderness of temptation.

The journey has but one guarantee: Christ promises to go with us and to bring us out the other side. Our Lord finishes what He starts. He does not abort His handiwork in the middle of its creation. He does not leave us staring at walking trees.

No, the Lord is intensely interested in our welfare and our maturing. He wants us to learn more and more about God and how to please God. He wants us to find joy in pleasing God. He wants us to change, like the healed blind man, so that our vision clears, so that we grow in how we perceive the world and how we act in it. Growth and change in such perception means learning more and more about what pleases the holy God. The growth in pleasing God is sanctification, and that is what this book is all about.

CHAPTER TWO
THE GOAL OF
CHRISTIAN LIVING

I once read the following definition of a fanatic: "A fanatic is a person who, having lost sight of his goal, redoubles his effort to get there." The fanatic runs around frantically getting nowhere. He is a basketball player without a basket, a tennis player without a net, a golfer without a green.

For a Christian to make progress in sanctification, in learning to please God, he must have a clear idea of what his goal is. Though the Bible makes that goal clear, it is one that is easily forgotten.

What is the goal? Jesus stated it this way: "Seek first the kingdom of God and His righteousness, and all these things shall be added to you" (Matthew 6:33).

Let us examine the elements of this charge. First, Jesus said that we must *seek*. To seek something requires effort. It involves a diligent search. It is like the woman who lost a coin and swept every nook and cranny of the house to find it. Seeking is not accomplished by taking a nap. It involves work. Persistent work. We do not sit back and wait for God to drop it in our laps.

We all know the story of the Greek mathematician Archimedes who discovered his famous principle of specific gravity while taking a bath. He shouted, "Eureka, I have found it." We also know the legend of Isaac Newton's discovering the law of gravity while sitting under an apple tree when an apple fell on his head. These flashes of insight that befell Archimedes and Newton were merely the culmination of years of diligent quest. Their achievements were not a matter of luck. It is said that Thomas Edison experimented with over a thousand different substances before he finally discovered one that would act as a suitable filament for the electric light. Not much luck, but much work. So is it with us in our learning to please God.

We are to seek the kingdom of God and God's righteousness. We notice that Jesus says that we are to seek these things *first*. The New Testament word that is used here for *first* is the Greek word *protos*, which does not mean simply first in a series of many things. Rather the word carries the force of *priority*. A more accurate translation of the concept would be, "Seek ye first, *above all else*, the kingdom of God and His righteousness."

Seek the kingdom. Seek righteousness. These are the priorities of the Christian life.

SEEKING THE KINGDOM OF GOD

What does it mean to seek the kingdom of God? There is much confusion about spiritual seeking in the Christian world. We frequently hear this comment out of the mouths of Christians: "My friend is not a Christian, but he's seeking."

What is the non-Christian seeking? One thing we know he is not seeking. He is not seeking God. Paul declares, "There is none who seeks after God" (Romans 3:11). The unbeliever never, never, never seeks God. The unbeliever is a fugitive from God. The natural pattern for man is to run from Him, to hide from Him. Jesus came to seek and to save the lost. He is the Seeker; we are the ones who are running. In man's sinful state he may look for answers to life's puzzles, but he does not seek God.

Why then does it so often seem to us that unbelievers are seeking God? We observe them. They are seeking happiness, peace of mind, relief from guilt, a meaningful life, and a host of other things that we know only God can give them. But they are not seeking God. They are seeking the *benefits* of God. Natural man's sin is precisely this: He wants the benefits of God without God Himself.

I belabor this point for this reason: Seeking after God is a Christian enterprise. The seeking of God *begins* at conversion. Though we may proclaim to the world that we "found it," the finding of God is, ironically, the beginning of seeking after God. To seek God is a lifelong pursuit. The seeking after God is what Jonathan Edwards called "the main business of the Christian life."

To seek God's kingdom is to fulfill the last command of Jesus as well as the crucial petition of the Lord's Prayer: "Your kingdom come. Your will be done on earth as it is in heaven."

The last question His disciples asked Jesus was, "Lord, will you at this time restore the kingdom to Israel?" (Acts 1:6). Just moments before Jesus departed this planet in His glorious Ascension His students pressed Him with one last question. The question was about the kingdom. Jesus answered the question first with a mild rebuke and then with a command: "You shall be witnesses to Me" (Acts 1:8).

We are called to seek the kingdom by bearing witness

to the kingdom. We are to seek to show the world what the kingdom of God looks like. For the kingdom to come on earth as it is in heaven means that loyal children of the King do the King's will here and now. We bear witnesses to God's kingdom by serving God's King. This is the will of God. This is what pleases Him. There is a reason why Jesus links the coming of the kingdom with the doing of the will of God. "Your kingdom come. Your will be done" belong together. They are two sides of the same coin. The kingdom comes on earth where God's will is done on earth.

The conclusion we reach is this: The great overarching goal of the Christian life is *obedience to the King*. And he is pleased when we obey.

SEEKING RIGHTEOUSNESS
The quest for the kingdom is linked with the quest for the righteousness of God. It is the kind of righteousness displayed by Jesus Himself. Jesus' life was a blaze of righteousness. He was the Lamb without blemish, the Son of whom the Father was well pleased. The Scriptures say of Him that zeal for his Father's house consumed Him (John 2:17). His meat and His drink was to do the will of His Father (John 4:34). Jesus was not only Incarnate God but was also the supreme man of righteousness. We cannot possibly imitate His deity, but we are to imitate His single-minded devotion to obedience, His commitment to pleasing God.

When I first became a Christian I was introduced to the priorities of the Christian community. I learned quickly that it was expected of me that I have a daily devotion time, a time reserved for Bible reading and prayer. I was expected to go to church. I was expected to have a kind of piety that was evident by not cursing, not drinking, not smoking, and the like. I had no idea that biblical righteousness went far beyond these things. However, like most new Christians, I learned to emphasize such things. My personal letters took on a new pattern of language. They began to sound like pages from New Testament epistles. I soon learned to use Christian jargon in my everyday speech. I didn't "tell" anybody anything, I "shared" it with them. Every good fortune was a "blessing," and I found I could hardly speak without sprinkling my sentences with spiritual platitudes.

Soon, however, I found that there was more to the Christian life than daily devotions and sanctified words. I realized that God wanted more. He wanted me to grow in my faith and obedience, to go beyond milk to the meat. I also discovered that Christian jargon was an almost meaningless form of communication, both to non-Christians and Christians alike. I found myself more interested in echoing a subculture's lingo than in finding true godliness.

My error was this: I was confusing spirituality with righteousness. I also discovered that I was not alone in this. I was caught up with a crowd who confused the means with the end. Spirituality can be a cheap substitute for righteousness.

Over the years I've had many young Christians ask me how to be more spiritual or more pious. Rare has been the earnest student who said, "Teach me how to be righteous." Why, I wondered, does anybody want to be spiritual? What is the purpose of spirituality? What use is there in piety?

Spirituality and piety are not ends in themselves. In fact they are worthless *unless* they are means to a higher goal. The goal must go beyond spirituality to righteousness.

Spiritual disciplines are vitally necessary to achieve righteousness. Bible study, prayer, church attendance, evangelism, are necessary for Christian growth, but they cannot be the final goal. I cannot achieve righteousness without spirituality. But it is possible to be "spiritual," at least on the surface, without attaining righteousness.

Jesus was a man of prayer. His prayer life was intense and powerful. He was a man of vast knowledge of the Scriptures. He obviously mastered the Word of God. He was spiritual. But His spirituality ultimately showed itself by authentic righteousness. So His spirituality was not merely a surface thing. His inner life displayed itself in outward obedience, obedience even unto death.

What is righteousness? The simplest answer to that question is this: *Righteousness is doing what is right in the sight of God.* This is a simple definition that is far more complex under the surface. To be righteous is to do everything that God calls us to do. The demands of true righteousness are so great and so many that none of us ever in this world achieves it perfectly. It involves following the whole counsel of God.

There are times when Scripture provides a simple summary of true righteousness. There are occasions when God reduces the vast sum of commandments to a few that capture the essence of true righteousness. Let us examine a few of those summaries.

MICAH'S SUMMARY

In the book of the prophet Micah we read this summary statement on holy living:

He has told you, O man, what is good; and what does the LORD *require of you but to do justice, to love kindness, and to walk humbly with your God? Micah 6:8,* NASB

Justice, kindness (or loyal love), and humility. This triad is not easy to achieve. God wants me to care about the weighty matters of justice and mercy. He enjoys the companionship of humble saints. He promises to add grace to the humble and to resist the proud.

Charles Colson had recently been released from prison after spending time incarcerated for his part in the Ellsberg paper incident. Though not part of the Watergate scandal, Colson was linked to the episode that brought about the downfall of Richard Nixon. Colson was speaking on a university campus and was being heckled unmercifully by some anti-Nixon students. One of the students interrupted Colson's speech by shouting, "Hey, Colson, why did you stick by Nixon?"

Colson stopped his speech and looked at the heckler. He replied, "Because he was my friend."

With that answer the audience erupted in spontaneous applause. Though the audience despised the Watergate scandal and all that it involved, they appreciated a kind of loyalty that would allow a man to go to jail for the sake of friendship.

When Micah speaks of "kindness" he uses the Hebrew word for "loyal love." It is the kind of love God has for His children. It is a steadfast love, a love that endures. It is the kind of love that lasts. Though God hardly approves of everything His children do, He stands by them. That's a priority of Christian love.

My children do not have to earn my love. They can disappoint me, frustrate me, and even anger me, but their failures do not disqualify them from my love. The Prodigal Son's father never stopped loving him. I cannot always give my permission but I must always give my love. To endure in love is to imitate how God loves us even when we fail.

Loyalty. Kindness. These qualities are what makes it possible for Christians to keep moving in spite of our sin. To be a loyal friend requires more than blind acceptance. It requires patience, long-suffering, gentleness, the kind of fruit that flows from the Holy Spirit. It is because Christ is loyal to us that we are motivated to show that same kind of loyalty to others.

JESUS' SUMMARY

Jesus summarized the Christian life in the simplest summation of all: "Just as you want men to do to you, you also do to them likewise" (Luke 6:31). This we call the Golden Rule—the law of gold, a gold more precious than diamonds and rubies. Any child can recite the Golden Rule, but to make it an active part of daily living is no mean feat.

I hate petty criticism. I do not enjoy the company of nitpickers. Judgmental people are difficult for me to enjoy. I cannot control how such people relate to me, but I can learn from them. From everyone who hurts me I can learn what kinds of things are hurtful. Chances are that what hurts me is the same kind of behavior that hurts other people. Therefore, I can learn what not to do to others.

Our response to petty criticism is often to retaliate in kind, instead of in kindness. This is where the Golden Rule touches life. Here is where Jesus spoke of not returning evil for evil. Doing to others what we want others to do to us is simply a matter of kindness. It involves being thoughtful and considerate. But it is more than mere politeness. It is doing what is right. It is doing what pleases God.

Righteousness means right living. It means treating people right. It means living with personal integrity. A righteous person is one whom we can trust. His integrity is consistent. It is not for sale. A righteous person is moral without being moralistic. He is pious without being pietistic. He has a sense of concern for other people's feelings. He wants to treat people right because he has the overarching desire to please a loving God.

37

JAMES' SUMMARY

The author of the Letter of James was probably the blood brother of Jesus. He was called "James the Just" or "James the Righteous" in the early church. His summary of true righteousness may be shocking to some Christians:

This is pure and undefiled religion in the sight of our God and Father, to visit orphans and widows in their distress, and to keep oneself unstained by the world.
James 1:27, NASB

True religion means visiting orphans and widows. Why does James say this? He understood that true righteousness is *people-oriented*. Our prayers are worthless if they do not result in the care of people. In the ancient world the orphan and the widow were almost helpless in society. They had financial stress, legal impotency, and, above all, the emotional stress of the pain of loneliness.

We now have government programs to aid orphans and widows financially. They have some legal rights. But the estate of widowhood or orphanhood is still not pleasant. They—and all other people who are lonely and helpless—still need the outreach of love. Societal institutions may change, but the requirement to show compassion to those in need stays the same. Piety without compassion is a lie. It turns the Golden Rule into rust.

We please the loving God when we obey the Golden Rule. We please Him when we pursue justice and mercy and when we practice loyal love. We please Him when we treat others as we wish to be treated. We please Him when we reach out to the forgotten and the downtrodden.

These, rules of Scripture for righteous living, weigh far more than concerns about a "spiritual" life that precludes drinking, smoking, and cursing.

Righteousness has rules, but it is more than rules. If we care for rules without caring for people, we have missed the goal of righteousness. The scriptural rules come from God precisely because He cares about people.

We need rules to be righteous, but they must be the right rules. They must be God's rules. We may accept no substitutes. In God's Word we find adequate rules for pleasing God with a righteous life. And if we abide by those rules, we are not goal-less fanatics, but true children of the King.

CHAPTER THREE

BEWARE THE
LEAVEN OF THE
PHARISEES

"**B**eware!" This is an ominous warning. It is the warning Caesar heard that made his bones tremble: "Caesar! Beware the Ides of March!" It is the warning the sailor Ishmael heard from the waterfront prophet before he signed on with the crew of the *Pequod* to join Ahab in his maniacal quest for Moby Dick.

The simple sign Beware of the Dog! is enough to give a burglar pause. The word *beware* posts a warning that stops us in our tracks, a caveat that conjures up visions of a menace that can quickly destroy or hurt us.

It was this word that Jesus used to startle His followers into vigilance against a deadly danger. "Beware the leaven of the Pharisees" (Luke 12:1, NASB). Jesus put up a signpost for the church, a divine call to heed the threat of a poison that could be swallowed by the unsuspecting. He warned of wolves in sheep's clothing, of rapacious killers that disguised themselves under the cloak of gentle spirituality.

The danger is one that kills by small doses. It is injected in seemingly harmless amounts, but it is potent in its full impact. "A little leaven leavens the whole lump," He said (1 Corinthians 5:6).

Jesus' words are a warning against allowing in an infectious element that can ruin the whole Christian life. It is something that rises from a small beginning. The warning is coupled with another frightening caveat. Jesus said,

"Unless your righteousness exceeds the righteousness of the scribes and Pharisees, you will by no means enter the kingdom of heaven" (Matthew 5:20).

If we fail to heed a Beware of the Dog sign, we may get bitten on the leg and get our pants ripped. But this warning of Jesus involves far more than a loss of some blood or a patch of our trousers. It means the loss of the kingdom of God.

What is this dreaded leaven of the Pharisees? In a word, it is the leaven of *hypocrisy.* It is the leaven of a false kind of righteousness. It is the leaven of deception, a masquerade of righteousness that is a substitute for the real thing.

"Unless your righteousness *exceeds* . . ." The word *unless* introduces a necessary condition for something else that follows. Here Jesus warns that our righteousness absolutely must surpass the righteousness of the scribes and Pharisees or we will miss the kingdom.

This warning is one of the most neglected warnings Jesus ever pronounced. It is lightly dismissed by the modern Christian, who sees no real threat in it. After all, what do we have to worry about? We view the Pharisees as the treacherous, corrupt group of unprincipled men who actually plotted the murder of Christ. What could be more diabolical than that? Surely it is a small thing for any lover of Christ to surpass Jesus' most hostile enemies in righteousness. The Pharisees have become the symbol of corruption to us. At first glance it would appear that the weakest Christian should have no problem in surpassing the Pharisees in righteousness.

We might offer an easy answer to Jesus' warning. We might ask, "What do we have to worry about?" As Christians we are justified by faith. By faith we receive the righteousness of Christ Himself. Surely Christ's righteousness surpasses the righteousness of the Pharisees. If we have the righteousness of Christ, what do we need to worry about?"

The easy answer is nothing! To be sure, if we truly have faith in Christ we do possess His righteousness. We are declared to be justified by God. The kingdom is ours. Nothing could be more certain than the fact that all who possess the righteousness of Christ will surely inherit the kingdom of God. Nothing more is required than the righteousness of Christ. No righteousness can possibly exceed that righteousness with which the Christian is cloaked by faith. In this sense the hymn writer was correct: "He's all I need."

That's the easy answer. The deeper question, however, still remains. How do I know I have the saving righteousness of Christ? Can I not deceive myself into thinking I have the real thing when in fact my faith is fraudulent? Just because a person claims to believe in Christ is no guarantee that he has saving faith. It is by our fruits that we demonstrate the reality of our faith. We know that God is pleased with those who truly honor Christ. We feel just as certain that He is not pleased when men blithely use the name but avoid any real life-affecting commitment to Him. This is the scary part of Jesus' warning.

BOTH THE WARNING AND THE DOG

There are homeowners who post signs saying Beware of the Dog when in fact they don't own a dog. They claim a dog when there is no dog. The warning has no reality to back it up. Jesus had harsh words to say about people who used words but had no reality to back them up. His words are a real threat to those whose righteousness is not genuine.

A local newspaper told an anecdote about a burglar who stalked the neighborhood watching for homes left unguarded by people leaving for vacation. He watched as a family loaded their suitcases into their car and departed. He waited until dark and then approached the front door and rang the bell. There was no answer. The burglar neatly picked the lock and let himself in. He called into the darkness, "Is anybody home?" He was stunned when he heard a voice in reply, "I see you, and Jesus sees you." Terrified, the burglar called out, "Who's there?" Again the voice came back, "I see you, and Jesus sees you." The burglar switched on his flashlight and aimed it in the direction of the voice. He was instantly relieved when his light revealed a caged parrot reciting the refrain, "I see you, and Jesus sees you." The burglar laughed out loud and switched on the lights. Then he saw it. Beneath the parrot's cage was a huge Doberman pinscher. Then the parrot said, "Attack, Jesus, attack!"

Jesus has the quintessential Doberman. His bite is worse than his bark. Jesus is really righteous, and so should His followers be. The sign Beware of the Dog points to a clear reality in His case. The words are not empty. There is a real dog on the premises, and He makes the sign very meaningful.

Beware of the Dog—a notice that is only valid if there is really a dangerous dog present. "We Christians, God's beloved children, have Christ's righteousness"—a valid statement only if we are truly aiming for righteousness. No pretense, just reality.

The fruit of our righteousness must exceed the pretense of righteousness displayed by the scribes and the Pharisees. On the surface the Pharisees achieved a high level of righteousness. Their righteousness was external. It was only an outward show. But their outward show was a brilliant display of virtue. It fooled a lot of people. Most tragically, it fooled the Pharisees themselves. They actually were able to convince themselves that they had the real thing. "Abraham is our father," they said (John 8:39). They claimed to be loyal to Moses. They were convinced they were in the kingdom. But they were not pleasing to God, who hates pretense.

Let us examine the level of righteousness the Pharisees achieved. We begin by noting that the Pharisees began as a kind of Puritan reform movement in Israel. There were no Pharisees in the Old Testament. They came into being in the period between the close of the Old Testament and the advent of the New Testament. They originated as a group of men who were concerned about the inroads of paganism into the Jewish nation.

Israel was being secularized. The Jews were moving away from fidelity and obedience to the covenant God had made with their fathers. The Pharisees were called

Pharisees because the word meant "separated ones." These men separated themselves from the trends toward paganism. They devoted themselves to the zealous pursuit of righteousness. They were almost fanatical in their drive to obey God. Their concern for godliness was neither casual nor superficial. They were seriously acting to please God.

The origin of Pharisaism was noble. But their movement soon degenerated into a kind of external pietism that was rooted in self-righteousness. They began to trust in their own good works, so that when their Savior came they not only missed His salvation but they plotted against Him. Their fatal error was this: They did not think they needed Christ. They thought they could please God without accepting the Redeemer He sent.

What were the Pharisees like in Jesus' day? What follows is a brief sketch of the marks of the first-century Pharisees.

THE PHARISEES WERE EVANGELISTIC

Jesus said to the Pharisees, "You travel over land and sea to make one proselyte, and when he is won, you make him twice as much a son of hell as yourselves" (Matthew 23:15).

Imagine the evangelistic zeal of people who would cross land and sea for one convert. This is missionary outreach of a higher order.

I hate to travel. I wish God would let me confine my ministry to my hometown. But I am required to travel great distances to carry out my work. When I am invited to speak, however, I usually consider the potential size of my audience before agreeing to travel. So far, I have not crossed the United States in order to preach to one person. I stand ashamed by the goal of the Pharisees in this regard.

They were evangelists. But Jesus marked them as evangelists of hell. They shame us in their zeal even as Mormons shame Christians and as communists tend to be more zealous for their cause than we do for ours.

But the warning is clear. Even though Christians are called to the evangelistic and missionary enterprise, the mere fact that we are involved in such work is no guarantee that we have exceeded the righteousness of the Pharisees. We should be alarmed if we are not zealous for evangelism and missions, but if we are, that does not in and of itself prove that our faith is genuine.

THE PHARISEES WERE TITHERS

On one occasion Jesus acknowledged that the Pharisees were scrupulous in their giving patterns. They did not fail to pay their tithes. Jesus noted this in the midst of proclaiming a curse upon them:

Woe unto you, scribes and Pharisees, hypocrites! For you pay tithe of mint and anise and cumin, and have neglected the weightier matters of the law: justice and mercy and faith. Matthew 23:23

The Pharisees fell into the trap of majoring in minors. Their priorities were reversed. Outward became more important than inward. They exalted minor matters to a high level in order to obscure their failure to be faithful in more important matters. But at least they paid their tithes.

In Israel the tithe was usually paid in terms of produce or livestock. The first fruits of their crops and herds were returned to the Lord. That the Pharisees were scrupulous about tithing is seen in Jesus' recognition that they even tithed from their mint and cumin. That would be comparable to a modern person who kept such strict accounts of tithing that when he finds a dime on the street he makes sure that he returns a penny to the Lord.

We could take a few lessons about tithing from the Pharisees. The latest survey I saw indicated that of those church members who identified themselves as "Evangelical" only 4 percent were tithers. If the survey is accurate, it would mean that 96 percent of evangelical Christians regularly and systematically rob God. In this area our righteousness falls short of the Pharisees. We might protest and say, "But we pay attention to the big things. We might not tithe but we are concerned about justice and mercy."

For the most part such protests are as hollow as they sound. We are called to be faithful in little things before we graduate to the big things. Even if it were true that we are so busy doing the big things that we have overlooked little things like tithing, it would not excuse us for robbing God.

On the other hand, if we are part of the small group who does tithe, we would have nothing of which to boast. We would simply be doing what it is our duty to do.

Tithing itself would be nothing greater than what the Pharisees did with scrupulosity.

Let me say again that we need to beware not only of the leaven of the Pharisees, but also to beware of judging the Pharisees too harshly. In their desire to please God they overemphasized the small (and visible) acts of righteousness. How tempting for us to so underplay these small acts that we end up neglecting both small and great matters. And if we neglect all, we are no more pleasing to God than were the Pharisees.

THE PHARISEES WERE MEN OF PRAYER

Jesus spoke of the Pharisees' pattern of prayer. They enjoyed making a public display of their piety. They assumed a reverent posture and offered eloquent prayers. They knew nothing of the kind of wrestling with God that characterized David's prayer life. Where David's pillow was wet with his tears, the pillows of the Pharisees were dry as a bone. And they had no prayer closet because a human audience could not fit in one.

The Pharisees piety was external. They were like the farmer in the story of a pig with a wooden leg:

A man and his wife returned home from church and enjoyed a Sunday supper. After dinner they decided to go for a ride in the country. During their leisurely tour the husband was startled to see a pig with a wooden leg in a pasture by the road. "Look at that!" he said to his wife. "There's a pig with a wooden leg!"

The man was amazed that a farmer would be so humane as to provide a wooden leg for his wounded pig. He insisted that they stop at the farmhouse and inquire about the circumstances that led to his porcine prosthesis. He knocked at the farmer's door and introduced himself to the farmer.

"I'm sorry to bother you, sir, but I am intrigued about the pig you have with a wooden leg. Would you mind telling me how it came about?"

"Not at all," said the farmer. "A few months back my grandchildren were here for a visit. One afternoon they wandered into a pasture where our bull was grazing. The bull charged them in fury. The pig noticed the danger and put himself between the children and the bull and headed the bull off. That pig saved my grandchildren's lives. The very next day one of the children fell in the farm pond and was drowning. That pig dove into the water and saved her life.

"So you see," said the farmer, "the pig is almost like family to us. That's why it has a wooden leg. I just couldn't bring myself to eat that pig all at one time!"

So much for the humane farmer. He wasn't *too* devoted to the heroic pig, but he at least wanted to *appear* grateful. The wooden leg symbolized, to passersby, the farmer's humaneness, but the passersby did not know the whole story. His concern for the pig was as deep as the Pharisees' real love for prayer. But at least the Pharisees prayed. They heaped up vain repetitions, but they at least went through the motions. Some of us have prayer lives that are so barren that we neglect even the motions of prayer. We displease God by hypocritical prayer, but we displease Him as well by our failure to pray.

THE PHARISEES READ THEIR BIBLES

Jesus rebuked the Pharisees by saying: "You search the Scriptures, for in them you think you have eternal life" (John 5:39). The Pharisees were learned in theology. They could recite chapter and verse of their Bible, the Old Testament. (They would have been champions in the "sword drills" so dear to Sunday school teachers!) But they missed the heart and soul of the Word of God.

But at least the Pharisees were diligent in searching the Scriptures. Many Christians never read the Bible. They have good intentions of reading it some day, but in the meantime they put it off. When theological disputes arise they may quote a text here and there, but there are few who embark upon a diligent *search* of Scriptures. We go to Bible studies where we have enjoyable fellowship, neat discussions, and tasty snacks. Often we do everything at Bible studies except study, and often when we do study, the word *superficial* seems to apply.

Jesus loved the Word of God. It was His meat and His drink. He calls His people to be diligent students of Scripture. But He demands more than the acquisition of Bible knowledge. We must have a sound doctrine of the Bible. But even this is not enough. The righteousness that pleases Him is a righteousness that proceeds from being doers of His Word and not hearers only.

Evangelism. Tithing. Prayer. Bible study. These are but a few of the rigorous activities of the scribes and the Pharisees. In all these things they excelled. But their activity was almost solely external. They were hypocrites. They went through the outward motions of piety, but their hearts were far from God. They kept the letter of the law but killed the spirit of the law.

The Scriptures warn us that man looks at outward appearances but God looks on the heart (1 Samuel 16:7). This is not to say that God cares only for the spirit of the law and not the letter. We cannot excuse external disobedience by appealing to a warm heart within. The Christian life that pleases God is one that is both internal and external. Authentic righteousness keeps the spirit and the letter. That kind of obedience exceeds the scribes and the Pharisees. It is the kind of obedience to which we are called.

CHAPTER FOUR

BATTLE WITH

THE WORLD

Martin Luther spoke of a threefold battle in the Christian life. The Christian is locked in combat with the world, the flesh, and the Devil. These are formidable opponents. They do not always fight fairly. It is a gang attack. The tactics of the enemy are devious. Satan is the master of the sneak attack. The flesh is an enemy within, a saboteur who undermines the Spirit.

In living to please a righteous God, we do constant battle with these enemies. Part of the process of sanctification is fighting with and—if we are truly growing—frequently triumphing over these foes. Every sensitive believer knows only too well how difficult it can be to win a victory against such formidable opposition.

In this chapter we will examine the first of the three enemies, the world. The world spirit, the value systems of a fallen creation, may be distinguished from the flesh and the Devil but not separated from them. The flesh is part of the fallen world and the Devil is the prince of this world.

We live in this world. We are part of the world. We are to a certain degree products of this world. And the world is our battlefield. The war is not contained in a European theater or Pacific theater. The world includes our own hometown. Wherever we live and move in this world, we are still engaged in combat. There is no demilitarized zone. The whole planet is fallen. The whole creation groans in travail waiting for redemption.

We live in a world injured by tooth, claw, and fang. We look forward to a new world where the wolf will lie down with the lamb and the child will play safely by the nest of the rattlesnake. But right now we do not invite wolves to act as shepherds of our sheep.

When I first moved to Florida, I quickly became aware of the danger of poisonous snakes. The dreaded eastern diamondback rattler thrives side by side with the menacing cottonmouth, or water moccasin. I was concerned for the safety of our grandchildren playing in our backyard. At the edge of my property I had a clump of palmetto palms that were overgrown with high grass and weeds. I was determined to clear the area lest it become a breeding ground for lethal reptiles.

As I began the task of clearing away the brush, my eye caught a sudden movement at the base of a palmetto. I was mesmerized by the appearance of a snake. It was beautiful—slender, graceful, marked with vividly colored rings of black, yellow, and red. The snake slithered away from me, appearing harmless. It looked like a living necklace, the kind of trinket that would surely attract the interest of an inquisitive child. But it was a coral snake, the most beautiful and most deadly of North American reptiles. I reacted in haste, moving quickly to destroy it.

Once the coral snake was dead, I put it in a jar and took it inside the house. There I showed it to the children and explained to them the danger the snake represented.

The world is filled with serpents of all varieties. The serpent that beguiled our first parents is still at large.

The venom of untamed creatures can spoil our garden. The world is indeed the habitat of devouring dragons.

THE SEDUCTION OF THIS WORLD

The world is a seducer. It seeks to attract our attention and our devotion. It remains so close at hand, so visible, so enticing. It eclipses our view of heaven. What is seen vies for our attention. It entices our eyes lest we look up for a better country whose builder and maker is God. It pleases us—much of the time, anyway—and, alas, we often live our lives to please it. And that is where conflict ensues, for pleasing the world so seldom overlaps with pleasing God.

The divine call we receive is this: "Do not be conformed to this world" (Romans 12:2). But the world wants us to be partners with it. We are urged to participate in the fullness of it. It presses upon us with the ultimate peer pressure.

Remember the anxiety we all experienced as teenagers? Our self-worth, our esteem, was measured by one magic word, a single all-encompassing standard: *popularity.* I remember going to a department store in Pittsburgh to buy shoes. I was in the sixth grade. My mother sat me down in the shoe department. While the clerk was showing me shoes, he asked me about my school. I blurted out, "I'm the most popular boy in my class!"

My mother was horrified. She lectured me on the virtue of humility. She explained that my boast was in the poorest of taste. No matter. What mattered to me was whether my words were true or not. I wanted to think I was the most popular boy in class. For my sixth-grade mind that was the central issue of life. Oh, to be sure, I wanted my parents to love me and my sister to be proud of me, but the end-all of my existence was popularity.

There was a price tag for popularity. I had to conform. I had to be "with-it." I had to wear the right clothes, learn how to comb my hair properly, know the lyrics to the right popular songs. To prove my masculinity I had to perform the proper rituals. I had to accept dares. I had to prove that I could "swipe" a magazine or a chocolate bar from the drugstore without being caught. I had to join in evening capers that involved being chased by the police. I had to commit pranks to harass my teachers. I had to learn the art of senseless vandalism. I cleaned out Mrs. Daughbert's onion patch and I didn't even like onions. I stole old Nick Green's grapes from his grapevine while Nick himself was busy picking grapes in the very next row. I learned how to copy Linda Huffington's homework and then pass it on to my buddies. These and many more antics were all part of the price for the mystique of popularity.

But that sort of thing passes with the passing of adolescence. Or does it? The games change. The tests are different. The price tags are different, for things are more expensive. But the stakes are the same. I still want to be popular.

In ninth grade I discovered a new way to be popular. Sports. I was the captain of the basketball team. My world pivoted on that axis. The Pittsburgh *Post Gazette* did not

cover our games. I did not make the cover of *Sport* magazine. But in my little world I was a hero. When we won,
I heard the cheerleaders: "Sproul, Sproul, he's our man, if
he can't do it, nobody can."

I loved the days at school following the nights when
our team won. As we walked the halls to change classes,
every student smiled at me and called me by name. In the
lunchroom the seventh-grade girls asked me to autograph
their napkins. When we won. But *only* when we won.

When we lost it was different. I lowered my head in
the halls to avoid the angry stares. I let tears escape from
my eyes and stain my pillow as I tried to fall asleep with
the sound of boos still in my ears. I didn't go to the
drugstore after the games we lost.

I learned very early not to trust the cheers of the
crowd. But I never learned to disdain them. They remain
a seductive force in my life. I still struggle to please men. I
still struggle with the mystique of popularity. I still hate to
be booed.

To be "conformed" to this world is to be *with* (Latin
con) the *forms* or *structures* of this world. It means doing
the popular thing. The conflict is this: What is popular
with men is not always popular with God. To be pleasing
to God is not always to be pleasing to men. Sometimes we
must choose whom we will please. That is a daily struggle
in the Christian life.

In every generation, every culture there is a dominant
prevailing spirit. The Germans coined a word for it, *Zeitgeist*, a term that joins two common ideas together. *Zeit* is
the German word for "time," *Geist* is the German word

for "spirit." So *Zeitgeist* means "spirit of the time" or "spirit of the age."

The contemporary Zeitgeist in which the Christian lives is one of secularism. The emphasis is on this world, on this time. Little attention is given to things that are above and beyond this world. Eternity is rarely considered, save for brief moments at a graveside. What counts is the here and now. To live for the moment, for the gusto of the present, is the spirit of this world.

The secular spirit of this world has its own modern trends and emphases, but in its essence it is not new. Every generation has its own form of secularism. We are earthbound creatures. Our focus is on this world.

The same was true in Jesus' day. He repeatedly called His disciples to look beyond the present. He lifted our gaze to the eternal. "Store up treasures in heaven," He said. He called us to weigh the matters in the balance of eternity. "What is a man profited if he gains the whole world, and loses his own soul?" (Matthew 16:26).

The world or the soul? Please the world or please God? This is the issue of every generation. To be conformed to this world is to risk the loss of one's eternal soul. The world places little value on the soul. A body in the hand is worth two souls in the bush, according to the Zeitgeist of our generation. The world spirit invites us to play now and pay later, though the emphasis is on the now. This is the popular way to go.

For the Christian to resist the seduction of this world he must risk going against the tide. He must be willing to risk the loss of pleasing men to gain pleasing God. Hence

Jesus said, "Blessed are you when they shall revile and persecute you, and say all kinds of evil against you falsely for My sake. Rejoice and be exceedingly glad, for great is your reward in heaven" (Matthew 5:11-12).

The key words in this beatitude are "for my sake." The nonconformity we are called to is not simply nonconformity for nonconformity's sake. Anyone can call attention to himself by being a maverick. It is the "for my sake" that separates cheap nonconformity from the genuine article. There is no virtue in being "out of it" indiscriminately. Our nonconformity must be *selective*. It must be at the points that matter.

It is easy to trivialize nonconformity. We can reduce this to simplistic externals as the Pharisees did. Authentic nonconformity rests upon transformation. The apostle Paul adds a positive mandate to the negative prohibition. He said, "Do not be conformed to this world, but be transformed by the renewing of your mind" (Romans 12:2).

It is the prefix that must be changed. The prefix "con-" ("with") must yield to the prefix "trans-," which means "across," "beyond," or "over." It is not enough for Christians to drop out of society. The call to transformation does not mean withdrawal from the world. We need no more monasteries. We are to go beyond the forms of this world. We are to effect changes in the world. The perspective of Jesus is beyond the forms of this world. We neither surrender to the world nor flee from the world. We are to penetrate the world with a new and different spirit.

There is a timeworn Christian saying that has become a cliché through its use: "We are to be in the world, but not *of* the world." To be *of* the world is to be worldly. It is to conform to this world. To drop out of the world is to be a nonconformist without transformation.

The theater of God's redemption is this world. It is to this world that God came in Christ. Christ refused to allow His disciples to hide in an upper room with the doors locked by reason of fear. No booths were allowed to be built on the mountain of Transfiguration. We are called to be Christ's witnesses in Jerusalem, Judea, Samaria, and to the ends of the earth. Jerusalem is in this world. Judea is in this world. Samaria is in this world. The ends of the earth are still on this earth. So we should not flee this world. But, oh, how many Christians try to do so. And in doing so, they may actually be displeasing the God who wants the world to be redeemed, not escaped.

THE EVANGELICAL FLIGHT

A great movement is sweeping the United States. The Christian parochial school has arisen as an alternative to secular public education. Christians are no longer satisfied to have their children educated by the secular state. The government has no zeal in inculcating a Christian world-view in public education. The state prefers to remain "neutral" with respect to the things of God. In the attempt at religious "neutrality," the schools educate children as if there were no God or as if God is not relevant to reading, writing, and arithmetic. But Christians know that there is little difference between an irrelevant God and no God at all.

The God of Christianity is the Creator of the whole world. He is sovereign over everything He creates. He is sovereign over the church *and* the state. He is sovereign over theology and over biology. So a "neutral" educator is an unvarnished myth. Every teacher and every curriculum has a viewpoint. Every teacher and every curriculum has a value system. Either God is integral to that viewpoint or He isn't. There is no neutrality with God. He is either acknowledged or He is ignored. Either way, a viewpoint is expressed.

More and more Christian parents are realizing that training a child in the things of God is a sacred duty. They are taking advantage of the limited freedom that remains in America for alternative education to the so-called neutral system. It means paying double, for the tax-collector still demands that we underwrite the state schools. Then we must pay again for our own educational system. It is hard to fault dedicated parents for putting forth so much effort—and money—to educate their children in an environment where pleasing God is a high priority.

But it is not good enough for schools to be mere nonconformists. The Christian school movement can be, and often is, merely a new form of monastic retreat, an attempt at insulation from the world with no witnessing to it. If we wish to please God, we must keep ourselves stainless, but we must do more than withdraw.

Some people have raised questions about just what makes Christian schools distinctively Christian. Merely teaching Bible classes or having prayer in classes does not make a school Christian. It is the perspective of the curriculum that counts. God must be acknowledged in every field of inquiry. And we must still study the world if we are to be effective witnesses in the world.

Recently, I received a telephone call from the headmaster of a Christian high school. He was facing a crisis that threatened to destroy his school. The senior English class included John Steinbeck's *The Grapes of Wrath* on its required reading list. Several parents were outraged by the selection and demanded that the book be removed from the list. Steinbeck's work was too "worldly" for the parents' taste. They did not want their children exposed to this type of literature. The parents insisted that only *Christian* literature be read in the course.

"What shall I do?" asked the headmaster. "How can we have an authentic course in American literature if we delete all non-Christian books from our reading list?"

The answer is simple. The school cannot have an authentic course in American literature if non-Christian books are excluded. If a student is to become knowledgeable of American literature, he cannot completely bypass Steinbeck or Hemingway or a host of other authors who are not Christian. Authentic Christian education is not "hot house" education. For a student to understand the major themes of the literature that shapes the American culture, he must be able to study them. What better environment to study the world's perspective than a school that acknowledges and honors God? To ignore such literature is to ignore some of the beauties of the world—and, yes, there are many—and to give ammo to critics who accuse Christians of being anti-intellectual and backward.

The apostle Paul was versed in worldly literature. At Mars Hill, as he debated with pagan philosophers, he quoted from the writings of pagan poets. (See Acts 17:28, where Paul quotes the poet Epimenides.) Paul did that not because he was worldly, but because he was educated. No one ever loved the Scriptures more than Paul, except for Jesus. Yet Paul found the time to read other things as well.

Augustine, bishop of Hippo in Africa, ministered to the church by virtue of his background in Neoplatonic philosophy. The great medieval theologian Thomas Aquinas answered the worldly philosophers of his day. John Calvin quoted Cicero almost as frequently as he quoted Augustine. Jonathan Edwards, who liked the writings of the philosopher John Locke, engaged the continental atheists with his pen. Those men were acutely aware of worldly philosophy and sought to defeat it with Christian truth. They did not retreat into an isolationist posture. At times, though they maintained a distinctively Christian stance, they quoted with approval the words of unbelievers.

There are risks involved in exposing our children to pagan thought. My own son was reading Aldous Huxley at age twelve. But he was reading him with my supervision. We discussed the ideas of the pagan philosophers together. We tried to examine the antithesis that exists between the perspective of this world and the perspective of the Word of God.

Some will reply: "But doesn't the Bible say that we

must 'beware of vain philosophy'?" (Colossians 2:8). Indeed it does. But to be able to beware of something we must first be *aware* of it. Authentic Christian education is not intimidated by worldly philosophers. We are confident that Christian truth goes beyond it. It triumphs over it. We need not flee from the enemy, nor do we need to compromise with the enemy. But it is to our advantage to understand how the enemy thinks.

I recently spoke with an executive of a Christian college. He made an unsettling remark: "The contemporary student has two options, a Christian education or a good education." The remark was not made in a spirit of cynicism. Rather, it was an expression of deep concern that Christian education not be satisfied with low standards of excellence. Many bright young Christians have gone to secular schools because they believed that they could receive a better all-around education there. Regrettably, their decisions have some basis in fact, although, thankfully, there are many excellent Christian colleges around.

God demands a transformed mind. This is a mind that views the world from a different perspective. We still study pagan philosophers. But we learn to "read with a comb"—that is, we have a value system that gives us the ability to be *critical* of what we study. Here the word *critical* does not mean coming with a negative spirit. It means to be cautious, to be discerning. The truth of God is the grid by which we are to evaluate the teaching of this world.

The call to transformation is a call to the renewal of the mind. The new mind comes from a deep study of God's perspective. That does demand a mastery of sacred Scripture. The Scriptures reveal the mind of God. The more we understand the mind of God, the less threatened we will be by Ernest Hemingway or Jean-Paul Sartre.

We can also learn something from the world. Not all of God's revelation is found in Scripture. God also reveals Himself in nature and in human culture. All truth is God's truth. Though in general the worldly philosophers are false prophets, not everything they say is false. Truth can be found anywhere. We can discover elements of truth in the writings of pagans. The nuggets of truth gleaned from them may be difficult to find, but they are there and we can benefit from them. Most books of sermon illustrations quote from unbelievers as well as from believers.

The world is an obstacle to our sanctification. But it can also be an ally if we approach it from the right perspective. This is still my Father's world. He does not despise it. He loves it enough to redeem it. He visits it. He does not abandon it, neither does He surrender it. At this point we must be imitators of God, seeking to approach the world in the same manner as He does. The goal is transformation.

We must learn how to live with the world and in the world as God's people. Martin Luther described a pattern of Christian growth that is helpful. He said that when a person is first converted to Christ he goes through a period of withdrawal from and renunciation of the world. The new convert in a real sense is "finished with the world." The old patterns of conformity must be set aside. There is a period of withdrawal during which we immerse ourselves in the things of God. Before Paul was sent out as the apostle to the Gentiles he first spent time in retreat in Arabia. Moses was in the wilderness, alone with God before he was sent to Pharaoh's court.

This period of withdrawal is both normal and healthy. But, as Luther insisted, we do not reach spiritual maturity until we are able to reenter the world, to embrace it, not as we once did in all its worldliness—but to embrace it as the arena of redemption. It is our place of labor. It is the place God made and to which Christ came. We do not give up on the world. In all of its fallenness, it is still our Father's world.

We must learn to claim it for Him. Not by conformity, not by yielding to its seduction, but by witnessing to it and transforming it. This can be accomplished without fear if we come to the world with minds that are renewed.

A renewed mind is essential in pleasing God. The God who desires our sanctification also desires that we shine like stars in a fallen world. We do this best when we understand this world and its values. When we understand—when we begin to perceive the world as God perceives it—then we can act with good conscience in renewing a marred creation. And in this we please the Creator and Redeemer.

CHAPTER FIVE
THE BATTLE
WITH THE FLESH

"The spirit indeed is willing, but the flesh is weak" (Matthew 26:41). This sentiment expresses a deep struggle that is a reality for every child of God. The New Testament speaks of a warfare between flesh and spirit. The flesh is part of Luther's triad of enemies, the world, the flesh, and the devil.

What then is the "flesh" of which Scripture speaks? What is there about the flesh that can lead a believer away from a God-centered, God-pleasing life?

THE FLESH—PHYSICAL OR FALLEN?

When we use the word *flesh* we usually mean our physical nature. On the one hand, flesh refers to the substance that composes our bodies. We speak of "flesh tones," of people appearing "in the flesh," of "suntanned flesh," of "flushed flesh," of "flesh and blood," and of kinsfolk who are "my own flesh."

Because our human flesh is something physical, we are tempted to see the biblical struggle between flesh and spirit as referring to a war between the body and the soul. But this is misleading. In biblical terms, *flesh* sometimes refers to the body and sometimes to something else. We will try to sort out the different ways in which the Bible speaks of flesh.

In the New Testament we find two Greek words that are often translated by the English word *flesh*. Those two

Greek words are *soma* and *sarx*. The word *soma* is normally used to refer to the physical body. (We have the
word *psychosomatic* as an integral part of the English
language. It combines the words for flesh or body—
soma—and mind—*psyche*.) Normally the word *soma* in
the Greek New Testament carries no connotation of sin-
fulness or fallenness. It is simply the word used to refer to
the physical body.

It is a different story with the Greek word *sarx*. Sometimes the word clearly refers to the physical body, but at
other times it means something else. It can either refer
simply to the physical flesh (just as *soma* does) or it can
refer to man's fallen nature.

When the Gospel of John declares, "The Word became flesh, and dwelt among us" (John 1:14), it does
not mean that the Word became fallen. It simply means
that the eternal Logos, the Word, took upon Himself a
human nature. The Word becomes *incarnate*. Likewise,
Paul speaks of his kinsmen "according to the flesh" (Romans 9:3). Here he is referring not to all of fallen humanity, but to his own ethnic group, the Jews. Paul's fleshy
kinsmen are his fellow Israelites. The apostle speaks in the
same manner as we do in describing our earthly relatives,
our "own flesh."

But there are special times in the Bible that *sarx* is used
to refer specifically to our fallen nature. Here *sarx* describes our corruption, which is by no means limited to
our bodies. The whole man is fallen. Sin infects every
aspect of our existence. By nature we have a "fleshly
mind" (Colossians 2:18). Neither the mind nor the flesh is

any less fallen than the other. They are both geared toward pleasing ourselves, not pleasing God.

A MIND OF FLESH

A "mind of flesh" does not refer simply to "evil thoughts about physical vices." The mind of flesh is a mind that involves a "mind-set" against God. It is the mind of a fallen humanity that does not want God in its thoughts. It is the mind of a person who is not guided by the Holy Spirit.

Paul expounds about an ongoing warfare between the flesh *(sarx)* and the Spirit *(pneuma)*. The contrast in Galatians 5:16-21 is not between man's spirit and man's flesh, but between the life led by the Spirit, the Holy Spirit, and the life that serves the flesh, man's fallen nature.

I say then: Walk in the Spirit, and you shall not fulfill the lust of the flesh. For the flesh lusts against the Spirit, and the Spirit against the flesh; and these are contrary to one another, so that you do not do the things that you wish. But if you are led by the Spirit, you are not under the law. Now the works of the flesh are evident, which are: adultery, fornication, uncleanness, licentiousness, idolatry, sorcery, hatred, contentions, jealousies, outbursts of wrath, selfish ambitions, dissensions, heresies, envy, murders, drunkenness, revelries, and the like; of which I tell you beforehand, just as I also told you in time past, that those who practice such things will not inherit the kingdom of God.

Here we see the stark contrast between flesh and Spirit. This is not a conflict between body and soul but between the old man who is driven by his fallen sinful nature and the new man indwelt by the Spirit of God. Here the Spirit and the flesh are opposed. They are in irreconcilable conflict. The flesh of our fallen nature resists the dominion of the Holy Spirit in our lives. The flesh takes offense at the Spirit and seeks to overcome it.

Likewise the Spirit is the enemy of the flesh. It wills what the flesh abhors. It wills righteousness. It seeks the fruit of the Spirit.

The contrast is seen vividly by two lists. The second list is well-known to Christians. It is the list of the fruit of the Spirit: love, joy, peace, and of such like. Our attention for the present, however, is on the first list. This list includes the work of the flesh.

As we examine the list of the works of the flesh one element is striking to us. The list includes sins that involve our bodies *and* sins that are of a more nonphysical character. In the list we find fornication and drunkenness. These are sins we commit with our physical appetites and bodily functions. Yet in this same list we find references to envy, jealousy, idolatry, and the like.

To be sure, when we are guilty of envy and jealousy, our bodies are involved. We don't do anything without our bodies. But envy is not a physical exercise. It involves a kind of mental attitude. It involves our minds, our thinking processes. We may use our bodies in acts of idolatry. We may physically bow down before an idol. But the essence of idolatry is not found in physical gestures but in the inward attitude of the heart.

We conclude then that when the New Testament speaks of flesh *(sarx)* in direct contrast to the Spirit *(pneuma)*, the primary reference of the flesh is not to our physical bodies but to our fallen sinful nature that includes the whole man. It is the conflict of two styles of living— the life of the flesh, which is controlled by the impulse to sin, and the life of the Spirit, which leads us into righteousness, into pleasing God.

CONTROLLED BY THE SPIRIT

This point is crucial to grasp lest we fall into the deadly error of thinking that righteousness consists chiefly in external physical acts. The kingdom of God involves much more than eating and drinking. If we focus merely on externals, we risk the trap of Pharisaism, which measures righteousness by outward, tangible actions. A saccharine smile can conceal an envious heart. A polite gesture can hide a jealous spirit. The Holy Spirit seeks to clean up our whole lives, both outwardly and inwardly.

At the same time we must guard against the opposite error of reducing righteousness to the internal realm. We can fool ourselves into thinking that all that matters is our inward attitude. As long as our spirit is right, it doesn't matter how we perform outwardly. This is an insidious form of self-deception. By it people seek to justify all sorts of sin. We say to ourselves that "love" justifies adultery. The teenager excuses his fornication by saying that it was committed in love.

It is also important to understand that though *flesh* does not exclusively refer to physical sins or inclinations, it does include them. They are powerful physical forces in our lives that are tainted by and influenced by our fallen sinful natures. Physical desires are often excruciatingly difficult to tame. These desires are not constant. They come in waves of varying degrees of intensity. It is easy to resolve to go on a diet *after* the dinner. It is another thing to go on a diet *before* dinner when hunger pangs are assaulting our wills.

The Spirit seeks to teach us self-control. We are called by God to harness our physical desires, to keep them in check. The desire to eat is, in itself, no sin. It is a normal physical function of our bodies. Yet when that desire runs out of control, we allow gluttony to enter our lives.

The sexual impulse is also a natural appetite that is not wrong in itself. God provides marriage as a context in which sexual expression is not only permitted, but it is commanded. We have both conjugal rights and conjugal responsibilities. Outside of marriage we are to abstain from sexual activities. God invented sex. God built the body with a complex of nerve endings that are highly susceptible to physical arousal.

It is possible that God could have made us with the ability to procreate without physical pleasure. He could likewise have made us with the ability to eat food without the added benefit of the pleasures of taste. But the Creator chose a more excellent way. Sex with all of its physical delight is a gift of God. But the gift comes to us with divine restrictions in its use. Sin is the abuse of the divine gift. It is using the gift in a manner God does not allow.

I once heard a man who was tragically involved in adultery declare, "My sexual organ has no conscience." He was excusing his physical behavior on the grounds that he was not personally responsible for what his body did. I explained that his sexual organ *did* have a conscience—his own mind. Our bodies are an integral part of ourselves. My whole body is to be governed by my mind. My mind is to be governed by the Law of God.

There are involuntary physical impulses. We do not cause our hearts to beat on rhythm by our ethical ideas. But not all of our bodily activities are involuntary. We are called by God to control our sexual behavior. We may not be able to control our awareness of what is sexually desirable, but we can control what to do about it.

Luther once observed some aspects of the question of lust. Lust is not noticing that a woman is sexually attractive. Lust is born when we turn a simple awareness into a preoccupied fantasy. When we invite sexual thoughts into our minds and nurture them, we have passed from simple awareness into lust. Luther put it this way: "We cannot help it if birds fly over our heads. It is another thing if we invite them to build nests in our hair."

Self-control is the rule of sexual activity. We are responsible to God for our sexual behavior. The Scriptures declare, "But fornication and all uncleanness or covetousness, let it not even be named among you, as is fitting for saints" (Ephesians 5:3). This absolute prohibition has been attacked by every subtle excuse known to man. The psychiatrists tell us that fornication among red-blooded youths is natural and normal. They are partly correct in their assessment. It is natural in the sense that by nature we are inclined to such activity. It is normal by virtue of the high statistical frequency of it. We could say that fornication is natural to normal *fallen* humanity. But so is lying. God forbids both.

It may be extremely difficult for a person to remain chaste, particularly in a culture where sexual taboos have been lifted and our senses are bombarded daily by erotic stimuli. But the Law of God is clear. He says, "No!" He calls us to self-control even in the midst of a fallen culture.

Consider for a moment the plight of the person with a homosexual orientation. This person suffers from a serious dilemma. God simply does not permit sexual acts between men and men or between women and women. Just as a heterosexual person is commanded to refrain from sexual activity outside of marriage, so the homosexual person is likewise called to chastity. God gives no provision for homosexual marriage. The homosexual is called to the same chastity as a single heterosexual person is called. Chastity pleases God, even if it seems initially unpleasant to our bodies.

Sexual chastity is difficult to achieve because of the weakness of the flesh. But it is possible to achieve, and God commands us to achieve it. If we fail, we are guilty of sin. Though we must be patient with those who fall into sin, we do no one a service by changing the standards of God and bringing them down to our own feeble levels of performance. It is scandalous to God for us to seek to change His standards and call good evil and evil good.

The flesh is an ally with the world. It seeks its justification not from the righteousness of Christ but from the standards of this world. The flesh is allied with the world and the world is allied with Satan. Here the enemy seeks our destruction by calling us away from the Spirit to surrender to the flesh.

But the Spirit is the believer's ally. How sad that every day we are reminded of our minds' and bodies' alliance with this fallen world while we forget that the children of God also have the Spirit to help them. In a world where the flesh seems to rule human activity, the Spirit is still present, enabling God's people to please Him.

CHAPTER SIX
THE DEVIL

The world, the flesh, the Devil. Of this triad of enemies, the most formidable foe we have is the Devil. Satan is not merely our enemy: He is our archenemy. He is called the prince of darkness, the father of lies, the accuser of the brethren, and the beguiling serpent.

The apostle Paul warns us that our battle against the Devil's forces transcends the visible and tangible elements of this world: "We do not wrestle against flesh and blood, but against principalities, against powers, against the rulers of the darkness of this age, against spiritual hosts of wickedness in the heavenly places" (Ephesians 6:12). That is, in our lives of trying to please a holy God, we are warring against not only our own petty desires but some fearsome, terrifying forces.

The first point we must understand in combatting the Devil is that there really is a Devil out there. In many segments of society, and even of the church, the concept of a personal Devil is regarded as primitive mythology. I remember asking a class of students who were studying Western philosophy this question: "How many of you believe in a real personal Devil?" In this class of thirty students, three indicated that they believed the Devil was real. The other twenty-seven indicated that they considered the Devil a myth.

I then asked the class, "How many of you believe in the existence of God?" To my surprise, all thirty indicated that they believed in God. I proceeded to my next question:

"How many of you would be willing to define God as a spiritual being who has the ability to influence men for good?" They all were willing to allow the definition.

Then I asked, "Why is it that you affirm the existence of a spiritual being who has the ability to influence for good, but you deny the existence of a spiritual being who can influence us to evil?"

The basic response I got was this: "Modern science has made it impossible for educated people to believe in the Devil." I questioned this point by asking, "What discovery of modern science has made the idea of Satan no longer credible? Is it the second law of thermodynamics? Is it the laws that govern nuclear fusion or fission? What is it?"

At first my question was met with stony silence. No one could point to a specific scientific discovery that applied. Finally one student said, "The idea of a Devil seems to fit in the category of ghosts and goblins. How can anyone believe in a sinister fellow in a red flannel suit with cloven hoofs, horns, and a pitchfork?"

The student was not responding to the biblical image of the Devil. His idea of Satan was a caricature. His Devil was a fugitive from a Halloween party.

SATAN THE PROUD AND POWERFUL

Where did the idea of a red-flanneled, pitchfork-bearing Devil come from? The roots of this grotesque caricature of Satan are found in the Middle Ages. It was popular sport in medieval days to mock the Devil by describing him in ludicrous terms. There was a method in this madness. The medieval church believed in the reality of Satan. It was aware that Satan was a fallen angel who suffered from an overdose of pride. Pride was Satan's supreme weakness. To resist Satan, that proud but fallen creature, required fierce combat. The combat focused on Satan's most vulnerable point, his pride. The theory was this: Attack Satan at his point of weakness and he will flee from us.

What better way to attack Satan's pride than to depict him as a cloven-hoofed court jester in a red suit? These silly images of Satan were intentional caricatures. Unfortunately, later generations responded to the caricatures as if they were intended to be the real thing.

The biblical view of Satan is far more sophisticated than the caricature. The biblical images include that of an "angel of light" (2 Corinthians 11:14). The "angel of light" image indicates Satan's clever ability to manifest himself *sub species boni* (under the appearances of good). Satan is subtle. He is beguiling. The serpent in the garden was described as "crafty" (Genesis 3:1). Satan does not appear as a fool. He is a beguiling counterfeit. He speaks with eloquence. His appearance is stunning. The prince of darkness wears a cloak of light.

A second image we have of Satan is that of a roaring lion who goes about seeking whom he will devour (1 Peter 5:8). Notice that the same figure that is used for Christ, the *lion*, is used by Satan, the archetype of the Antichrist. The anti-lion devours. The Lion of Judah redeems.

With both allusions to the lion we find a symbol of

strength, though with Satan it is an evil, demonic strength. His strength is no match for Christ, but it is a strength that is certainly superior to ours. He is not as strong as Christ, but he is stronger than we are.

There are two frequent ways that Satan deceives us. On the one hand he will seek to have us *underestimate* his strength. On the other hand there are times that he seeks to have us *overestimate* his strength. In either event he deceives us and can trip us up.

The pendulum of popular belief about Satan tends to swing between two extremes. On one side there are those who believe that he doesn't exist at all, or if he does exist, he is a mere impersonal evil "force," sort of a collective evil that finds its origin in the sin of society. On the other side there are those who have a preoccupied fixation, a cultic focus of attention upon him that diverts their gaze from Christ.

Either way Satan gains some ground. If he can persuade people that he does not exist, he can work his wiles without being detected or resisted. If he can get people to become preoccupied with him, he can lure them into the occult.

Peter underestimated Satan. When Jesus warned Peter about his impending betrayal, Peter protested, saying, "Lord, I am ready to go with You, both to prison and to death" (Luke 22:33). Peter was overconfident. He underestimated the strength of the adversary. Moments before Jesus had warned him about the strength of Satan, but Peter rejected the warning. Jesus said, "Simon, Simon!

Indeed, Satan has asked for you, that he may sift you as wheat" (Luke 22:31).

Peter's protests notwithstanding, he became as putty in the hands of Satan. It was as easy for Satan to seduce Peter as it is to sift wheat in a sieve. In common jargon it was as if Jesus said to Peter, "Peter, you are a piece of cake. You are no match for the formidable strength of the Devil."

Even so, Satan's power over us is limited. He may be stronger than we are, but we have a champion who can and does defeat him. The Scripture declares, "Greater is He who is in you than he who is in the world" (1 John 4:4, NASB). James adds these words: "Therefore submit to God. Resist the devil and he will flee from you" (James 4:7). When we resist the roaring lion in the power of the Holy Spirit, he runs away with his tail between his legs.

Satan sifted Peter, but his victory was temporary. With the warning Jesus gave came also the consolation: "But I have prayed for you, that your faith should not fail; and when you have returned to Me, strengthen your brethren" (Luke 22:32). Jesus predicted both the fall and the restoration of Peter.

To underestimate Satan is to suffer from the pride that goes before destruction. To overestimate him is to grant him more honor and respect than he deserves.

Satan is a creature. He is finite and limited. He is subordinate to God. Christianity never embraces an ultimate dualism of equal and opposite power. Satan is stronger than men but no match for God. He has no divine attributes. His knowledge may exceed ours, but he is not omniscient. His strength may be greater than ours, but he is not omnipotent. He may have a wider sphere of influence than we have, but he is not omnipresent.

Satan cannot be at more than one place at one time. He is a space-time creature who is limited, as are all angels good or bad, by space and time. Chances are that in your whole lifetime you will never experience a direct, immediate encounter with Satan himself. You might encounter one of his junior-grade lieutenants or one of his host of disciples, but he is likely to spend his time and space in bigger targets than you or me. Even in his concentrated attack on Jesus, Satan departed from him "for a season" (Luke 4:13).

TOO MUCH CONCERN WITH DEVILS?

In our day there has been a renewal of interest in the work of Satan. Hollywood has given us *The Exorcist* and *The Omen* and a host of other films to whet our appetite for the occult. Within Christian circles there has arisen a new concern for ministries of deliverance. Some of these deliverance ministries have developed a bizarre and radically unbiblical view of demon possession and deliverance.

For example, we hear that we can recognize the departure of a demon from a human soul by a manifest sign that is linked to the particular point of bondage. We have people saying that particular demons cause particular sins. There is, they say, a demon of alcohol, a demon of depression, a demon of tobacco, and so on. I have listened to tapes from well-known deliverance ministers (whose names I will not mention, to protect the guilty) in which they teach the signs of departure of the demon. A sigh, for example, indicates the departure of the demon of tobacco. Since the tobacco demon enters with the inhaling of smoke, he leaves us with an audible exhale. Likewise vomiting may be the sign of the departure of the demon of alcohol. There are demons for every conceivable sin. Not only must each one of these demons be exorcized, but there are necessary procedures to keep them from returning on a daily basis.

I know of no polite way to respond to this kind of teaching. It is unmitigated nonsense. Nowhere in sacred Scripture is there to be found the slightest hint of this kind of demonic diagnosis. These teachings cross the line into the sphere of magic and result in serious harm to believers who are duped by them. Sadly, too much concern with Satan and demons means that we focus less of our attention on Christ. That must please Satan, though it certainly is not pleasing to God.

The Scriptures indicate that Satan can oppress us, assault us, tempt us, slander us, and accuse us. But a Christian who is indwelt by the Holy Spirit cannot be possessed by a demon. Where the Spirit of the Lord is, there is liberty. If a person indwelt by the Holy Spirit can at the same time be sovereignly controlled by an evil spirit, then our redemption is defeated.

All this emphasis on Satan and demons tends to distract us from another very real menace, our own sin. Yes, there is a Devil. There are real demons. But there is also the reality of sin. Satan may be our accomplice in our ongoing sin, but we cannot pass the blame and responsibility for our sin to a controlling demon. We do not have to be possessed by a Devil to get drunk. There is enough abiding wickedness in us to do it all by ourselves. We can never say, "The Devil made me do it." We can say that we are tempted or incited or seduced by Satan, but not that we are controlled or coerced by him.

There are two serious problems with the view that our sins are the result of controlling demons. The first is that we yield to the temptation to take no personal responsibility for our sin. How can we be responsible if in fact we are not able to resist? Second, we are lured into thinking that we are powerless without the aid of the deliverance minister. We are encouraged to think that we are not really guilty and that we are actually helpless without a minister with special powers of deliverance. This negates the entire biblical concept of sanctification. It is surely unbiblical to teach that we cannot lead lives pleasing to God unless some so-called expert on deliverance enters into the battle. Therefore, I say with all urgency that believers must turn away from those who teach such things. Indeed run, for your very spiritual lives.

THE TEMPTER AND ADAM

What then does Satan do to us? There are two chief activities with which Satan directs his power against us. These primary activities are temptation and accusation. We will look closely at accusation in the next chapter. Our concern here is his work as the tempter.

Satan's work of temptation is seen most dramatically in the Genesis account of the fall of Adam and Eve and in the wilderness testing of Jesus. Some startling parallels and contrasts may be observed in these two episodes.

In the Garden of Eden, the serpent approaches Eve with an innocuous-sounding question: "Has God indeed said, 'You shall not eat of every tree in the garden'?" (Genesis 3:1).

On the surface the question sounds silly. Satan assumes a pose of amazement, as if he is surprised by the severity of God's rules and prohibitions. "Did God really say that you are not allowed to eat of any of the trees of the Garden?" The question involved an obvious distortion. Eve was quick to set the Devil straight: "We may eat the fruit of the trees of the garden; but of the fruit of the tree which is in the midst of the garden, God has said, 'You shall not eat it, nor shall you touch it, lest you die' " (Genesis 3:2-3).

God had given Adam and Eve free use of the garden— with one exception. One tree was placed off limits. The rest were fully available. Yet Satan asked, "Did God say you couldn't eat from any of the trees?" Here we see the subtlety of the serpent. His thinly veiled suggestion is that if God places one limit on human freedom, he has taken away freedom altogether. The serpent's question was more than a question. It was an accusation against the fairness and kindness of God.

We see a parallel with our children's response to prohibitions. If our children ask permission to do ten things and for the first nine we say yes, but on the tenth we say no, the standard complaint is, "You never let us do anything!"

Adults are much the same way.

Satan's question is an indirect assault on the integrity of God. He moves quickly from an indirect attack to a frontal assault. When Eve sets the record straight and declares that only one tree is forbidden with the divine warning of death, Satan boldly declares: "You will not surely die. For God knows that in the day you eat of it your eyes will be opened, and you will be like God, knowing good and evil" (Genesis 3:4-5).

Here the temptation is wrapped in a bold-faced lie: "You will not die." The serpent declares a clear contradiction of what God said. Satan accuses God of lying. "You won't die. God says you will die, but I say you will not."

The issue is, who is telling the truth? Jesus called Satan "a liar, and the father of lies" (John 8:44, NASB). Satan's chief device of temptation is to attack the truth of God. Not only does Satan accuse God of lying, but he provides Eve with a reason for God's lie. He charges God with a kind of divine jealousy. God does not want Adam and Eve's eyes to be opened. He wants to keep His level of knowledge to Himself. He does not want to share His deity. He is afraid that the fruit of the tree will make Adam and Eve divine. His prohibition is both unfair and selfish.

Now Satan launches an all-out attack on the integrity of God. He is suggesting that Adam and Even have a *right* to the tree. God's rules are unfair. Man has an in-alienable right to do what he pleases, even if it is not pleasing to God.

This was not the last time in history such a temptation

was placed before man. The same diabolical train of thought takes place in the human mind every day. Every time I sin, I sin because I want to do what I want to do rather than what God wants me to do. Deep within our hearts we harbor the treacherous thought that God's laws are not fair.

THE TEMPTER AND CHRIST

Now consider the temptation of Christ. First, let us note the differences between the circumstances of the test of Adam and Eve and that of Jesus. Adam's temptation took place in the midst of paradise. He had the comfort of human fellowship. He had a full stomach. A gourmet feast was there for the taking. Adam had every creature comfort available.

By contrast Christ was alone. In solitude he faced the worst natural elements. The Judean wilderness was the habitat of scorpions, scrub brush, and a few birds. Devoid of human companionship, Jesus faced a temptation after forty days with no food. He had no fruit to eat, no trees from which to choose.

In spite of this stark contrast of circumstances, there was a striking similarity of the temptation. The same issue was at stake, the trustworthiness of the Word of God. The Devil approached Jesus and said, "If You are the Son of God, command this stone to become bread" (Luke 4:3). Notice that Satan did not say, "*Since* you are the Son of God . . ." The accent was on the first word: "*If* you are the Son of God . . ."

Why the *if?* What were the last words Jesus had heard before the Spirit drove Him into the wilderness to be tested? The heavens had opened at Jesus' baptism and God spoke audibly saying, "You are My beloved Son; in You I am well pleased" (Luke 3:22).

The subtle suggestion of Satan by using the word *if* was this: "Are you sure you are the Son of God? If you are so beloved of God, what are you doing here? Is this how God treats His Son in whom He is well pleased? Perhaps we need to make sure that you are the Son of God. You're hungry, aren't you? It shouldn't require much power from the very Son of God to change a few stones into bread. What harm will that do?"

Jesus was quick to reply. Of course He was hungry, but His hunger for righteousness was greater than His hunger for bread. His meat and His drink was to do the will of the Father. He said, "Man shall not live by bread alone, but by every word of God" (Luke 4:4).

Jesus saw through the subtlety of Satan's words. In Jesus' mind there was no "if." God had said that He was His Son. Jesus lived by the Word of God. Adam was enticed to deny the truthfulness of what God said. Jesus was not moved from it.

Satan changed his tactics with Jesus. He showed Him all the kingdoms of this world. He said to Jesus, "All this authority I will give You, and their glory; for this has been delivered to me, and I give it to whomever I wish. Therefore, if You will worship before me, all will be Yours" (Luke 4:6-7).

Power and glory. These were the enticements. Satan

was armed with this maxim: "Every man has his price." But he was unable to find a price for Jesus. This was the man without a price. This was the man who later would ask, "What shall it profit a man if he gains the whole world, and loses his own soul?" (Mark 8:36).

Jesus replied to Satan, "Get behind me, Satan! For it is written, 'You shall worship the Lord your God, and Him only you shall serve' " (Luke 4:8). Again the issue was the same: obedience to the Word of God. What Satan offered could only be accepted by Jesus if He was willing to negotiate the Word of God. Jesus repelled Satan with Holy Scripture. "It is written . . . ," said Jesus. He quoted from Deuteronomy. Obviously Jesus had more regard for the Pentateuch than many of our contemporaries. He had moments before declared that men must live by every word that comes from God. Then He cited a specific word that cannot be broken.

It was Satan's turn to quote the Bible. Again he used the word *if.* "If you are the Son of God, throw Yourself down from here. For it is written: 'He shall give His angels charge over you, to keep you,' and 'In their hands they shall bear you up, lest you dash your foot against a stone' " (Luke 4:9-11).

Satan was not above citing Scripture. His, however, was a distorted hermeneutic. He twisted Scripture by setting Scripture against Scripture. He appealed to the Bible as his source to justify sin. He did radical violence to the Holy Spirit.

It was as if Satan had said, "OK, Jesus, You say You believe the Scripture. Then prove it! Put God to the test.

Throw Yourself down and see if the angels will catch you."

Jesus replied, "It has been said, 'You shall not tempt the Lord your God' " (Luke 4:12).

What Jesus was saying is clear. "I know the promises of God. But don't try to tempt me with a promise that is circumscribed by a prohibition. The Bible also says that we must not put God to the test (Deuteronomy 6:16). I don't need to jump off the pinnacle of the temple to know that the angels are caring for Me. God has declared it and I am confident that what He has declared is true."

The irony of this reply is found in Matthew's Gospel: "Then the devil left Him, and behold, angels came and ministered to Him" (Matthew 4:11).

THE TEMPTATION TO UNBELIEF

In both cases of temptation, with Adam and with Jesus, the issue focused on the trustworthiness of God's Word. If Satan can cast doubt on the veracity of God's Word, the stage is set for our fall. Failure to believe what God says is the foundation of all sin. Once the truth of God is set aside, we have nothing to restrain us from doing what is right in our own eyes. Doing our "own thing" is the very essence of disobedience. And when we keep our attention focused on what is right in our own eyes, we cannot possibly be committed to pleasing God.

Why is unbelief a sin? To refuse to believe God is to be guilty of slandering His righteous character. It is to assume that either God does not know what He is talking about or that what He says is in fact evil. Either way we assault His divine integrity. Either His omniscience or His righteousness is brought into question.

But isn't blind faith a weakness? Indeed it is. There is a great difference between faith and credulity. Credulity is gullibility, naiveté. It is based on superstition and irrational prejudice. To believe something with no reason for believing is not a virtue. But God does not require that. He asks us to believe in that which He utters in the fullness of light and with consummate evidence. He does not ask us to believe in a Resurrection without first bringing Jesus forth from the grave.

He does ask us to trust Him for the future, but such trust is not blind. It rests upon God's perfect track record. He has demonstrated over and over that His promises are certain. Indeed, if we were asked to put our unquestioned trust in a man who has been repeatedly convicted of fraud, whose promises are constantly broken, who is a notorious liar and cheat, such trust would be incredulous.

But God is not a man. He is guilty of none of those things. We dare not transfer to God the same lack of integrity that we find in ourselves.

The Roman Catholic church has a concept that is worth our attention. It is the idea of a *fides implicitum*. This means simply that the believer is to give the church an implicit faith, or to trust the church implicitly because the church as an institution that teaches Christian doctrine is considered infallible.

Indeed, if the church were infallible it would be right and proper to grant it an implicit faith. Whatever or whoever is infallible deserves such trust. I don't believe that the Roman Catholic church or any church is infallible. But God is infallible. To Him we owe a *fides implicitum*.

If Satan can destroy our implicit trust in God, then his goal of seduction is achieved. We fall to the temptation of unbelief. Adam fell. He did not believe God. Jesus, the second Adam, lived by the Word of God. His trust in the Father could not be shaken. He did not yield to the tempter.

Before Jesus' temptation, He had heard the voice of the Father, who declared His approval of the Son: "I am well pleased." We can feel certain that God was also well pleased at Jesus' victory in the temptation. Jesus chose well between the word of Satan the liar and the Word of God. He cast His lot with trust and belief instead of selfish doubt and skepticism. Both then and now God takes pleasure in His children when they trust.

CHAPTER SEVEN

SATAN

AS ACCUSER

As powerful as Satan is in his work of temptation, he is also formidable in his work of accusation. In the last chapter we looked at how we please God by resisting Satan the tempter. Here we will look at how, at times when we do sin, we please God by throwing ourselves on His mercy instead of listening to the taunts of Satan the accuser.

THE SINISTER ACCUSER

As an accuser of God's people, Satan can disguise himself as the Holy Spirit and bury us in a quagmire of moral confusion. He can make us feel good when we should feel guilty and make us feel guilty when we should be at peace.

Zechariah records an incident that displays the accusation of Satan:

Then he showed me Joshua the high priest standing before the Angel of the LORD, and Satan standing at his right hand to oppose him. And the LORD said to Satan, "The LORD rebuke you, Satan! The LORD who has chosen Jerusalem rebuke you! Is this not a brand plucked from the fire?"

Now Joshua was clothed with filthy garments, and was standing before the Angel.

Then He answered and spoke to those who stood before Him, saying, "Take away the filthy garments from him." And to him He said, "See I have removed your iniquity from you, and I will clothe you with rich robes."

And I said, "Let them put a clean turban on his head." So they put a clean turban on his head, and they put the clothes on him. And the Angel of the LORD stood by.

Then the Angel of the LORD admonished Joshua, saying, "Thus says the LORD of hosts: If you will walk in My ways, and if you will keep My command, then you shall also judge My house, and likewise have charge of My courts; I will give you places to walk among these who stand here." Zechariah 3:1-7

Joshua was clad in filthy garments. As he stood in the presence of God, Satan called attention to his clothes. The enemy accused Joshua before the Lord. Indeed his clothes were dirty. Satan picked on a vulnerable spot. But the Lord defended His elect. "Is not this a brand plucked from the fire?"

Every Christian is a brand plucked from the fire. The salvaged brand is rescued from the inferno. After it is removed from the center of the flames, the heat can no longer destroy it. It may smolder for a few moments, but it survives.

A smoldering brand is filthy. It makes black marks on whoever handles it. Its charred surface is covered with tar and soot.

That is who we are. The redeemed of God who are snatched from the flames by the hand of the Lord are still covered with ashes. We remain streaked with charcoal. We remain blemished with soot. We are redeemed, but not totally sinless. Satan is quick to call attention to the dirt. He wants us to be more conscious of our own sin than of God's mercy.

Satan's accusations are met by a divine reprimand: "The LORD who has chosen Jerusalem rebuke you!" God stops the mouth of Satan. Christ is our attorney who rises to our defense. As Satan prosecutes us, Christ stands before the bench and declares, "Objection, your honor! This is one of My brands snatched from the fire." God replies from the throne of judgment, "Objection sustained!" The tongue of the accuser is silenced in the courtroom of the Almighty.

The Lord's angel removed Joshua's filthy garments and clothed him with rich robes. A clean turban was placed upon his head. This is how Christ clothes His redeemed. We are clothed in His righteousness so that we need not be embarrassed in the presence of God.

The right clothing can be so important. Recently I attended a reception for the governor of Florida. It was a black-tie affair and my invitation came at the last minute. I rushed to the tuxedo rental agency to order my outfit. The clerk put a rush order in but declared that my tuxedo might not arrive in time. That night I dreamed that I appeared at the reception without a tuxedo. I was the only person present who was improperly dressed. I awoke in a cold sweat and was instantly relieved that it was only a bad dream.

It is one thing to commit a social faux pas by being improperly dressed in front of the governor. It is quite another to show up in the presence of God dressed in filth. Rightly do we fear being poorly dressed in the throne room of God.

But God has His own private tuxedo shop. The clothes he puts on us are not rented. They are given to us permanently. To be sure, they conceal ragged undergarments, but we are properly covered. Once we are attired in these clothes we will never again suffer embarrassment. These garments never wear out; they never go out of style.

It was God who made the first suit of clothes. The first recorded act of divine mercy was God's providing clothing to cover Adam and Eve's nakedness. He had mercy on their shame and stooped to minister to their embarrassment (Genesis 3:21). He continues to provide garments for his beloved but sin-stained people.

Zechariah records that after the Lord removed Joshua's iniquity and put him in clean clothes He admonished him—that is, he reprimanded him in a kind, loving way. In this short episode Joshua experienced both the accusation of Satan and the admonishment of God. This is not unlike what we experience as Christians. When we sin we can receive both the accusation of Satan and the conviction of the Holy Spirit.

What is the difference? The goal of Satan's accusation is to harm us. He wants to drive us away from God. The goal of the Spirit's conviction is to turn us from sin. He wants our awareness of sin to bring us close to God. Satan would have us perish in our guilt. The Spirit seeks to save us from our guilt. They both may call attention to the same sin. But their goals are radically different.

THE SWEET CONVICTION

Satan's accusations drive us to despair, but there is something sweet about the conviction of the Holy Spirit. When He brings our guilt to our attention, He brings also the consolation of forgiveness and restoration.

Consider the experience of the prodigal son. After he had wasted his inheritance and was reduced to the ignominy of feeding swine, he reached the depths of coveting the pods that the pigs ate. Then, the Scripture declares, "He came to himself" (Luke 15:17).

To come to oneself is to awaken to one's desperate plight. It is to have a revival of conscience. The segment of the conscience that had been temporarily dormant is suddenly awakened. It is as though one awakens from a moral slumber. What follows is authentic remorse coupled with a resolve to cease from wickedness. The parable expresses it this way:

But when he came to himself, he said, "How many of my father's hired servants have bread enough and to spare, and I perish with hunger! I will arise and go to my father, and will say to him, 'Father, I have sinned against heaven and before you, and I am no longer worthy to be called your son. Make me like one of your hired servants.'" And he arose and came to his father. But when he was still a great way off, his father saw him and had compassion, and ran and fell on his neck and kissed him. Luke 15:17-20

Here we see the kind of result that follows from the conviction of God the Holy Spirit. When the Spirit convicts us of sin, He leads us to repentance and restoration.

The initial awakening to the reality of guilt may be painful, but it does not lead us to despair. Rather, it leads us back to the Father, who is eager to embrace us. The Father kills the fatted calf, clothes us with His finest robe, puts shoes on our blistered feet, and adorns our hand with the family ring. Certainly this parable makes it clear that nothing is more pleasing to God than our sincere sorrowing over sin and turning from it.

The Spirit's conviction is liberating. It is kind and gentle. The judgment is coupled with compassion. The welcome sign is vividly displayed for those with contrite hearts. It is a time not for bitter retribution but for godly merriment. There is rejoicing among the angels and delight in the heart of God. Observe the gladness of the father in the parable:

"And bring the fatted calf here and kill it, and let us eat and be merry; for this my son was dead and is alive again; he was lost and is found." And they began to be merry. Luke 15:23-24

The goal of Satan's accusation is not restoration but destruction. The last thing he wants to see is repentance. There is no joy among his lieutenants when a sinner comes to himself and quits his sin. Rather, Satan wants us to surrender to sin. He wants everybody in the pigpen. His torment aims at making the sinner bitter and hostile toward God. He wants the sinner to feel sorry for himself and to blame God for his plight. He would have hoped that while the son was busy cursing the pigs he would also curse God. He wanted to hear the prodigal say, "My father did not provide enough of an inheritance. God is not fair to allow me to be starving with pigs."

The attitude of Satan is mirrored in the attitude of the elder son:

Now his older son was in the field. And as he came and drew near to the house, he heard music and dancing. So he called one of the servants and asked what these things meant. And he said to him, "Your brother has come, and because he has received him safe and sound, your father has killed the fatted calf." But he was angry and would not go in. Luke 15:25-28

Here we see anger and jealousy toward the father's mercy. This was Satan's attitude toward Job. It is the Devil's mentality that seeks to accuse rather than forgive. This is why a judgmental spirit is unbecoming to a Christian. It is why the apostle Paul speaks so strongly of the strength we find in the stronghold of Christ:

Who shall bring a charge against God's elect? It is God who justifies. Who is he who condemns? It is Christ who died, . . . who is even at the right hand of God, who also makes intercession for us. Romans 8:33-34

Paul's questions are rhetorical. When he asks, "Who will bring a charge against God's elect?" he is saying, "Nobody dare!" To accuse one whom God has justified is to insult the gospel. To condemn one for whom Christ died and for whom Christ intercedes is as foolish as it is wicked.

Our defense against the accusation of Satan is the gospel. He despises the gospel. He denies the gospel. He wants us to seek our justification somewhere other than in our Christ, who clothes us with His perfect righteousness. Satan will lay charges against us. He will condemn us. He will shout into our ears that our garments are filthy, that we are too sinful to ever be pleasing to a righteous God. But in Christ we say, "Begone, slanderer—who shall bring a charge against God's elect? My Savior has covered me. He has taken away my iniquity. He prays for me at this very moment. Cover your ears, Devil, lest you hear the intercession of Christ for me. Christ is my righteousness. His merit is mine. Nothing can separate me from His love."

We please God when we resist temptation and do not sin. Certainly part of our maturing in the Lord is to do this more and more. But we do sin, again and again, and as we grow in the Lord we become even more conscious of how many ways we can find to sin against God and others. But part of our growth is becoming more and more sure of God's acceptance of us. He does not save us because of our spotless lives, but because we are clothed in Christ's righteous garments. Our awareness of our sin is painful indeed, but it is a sweet pain that drives us into the arms of the loving Father. We please Him when we do not leave His side, as Satan the tempter would have us do. We also please Him when we return to Him, something Satan the accuser does his best to prevent. When Satan whispers to the believer, "You, with all your sin, can't be pleasing to God," the believer replies, "Ah, but I am. To God be the glory."

CHAPTER EIGHT
FEAR AND
GUILT PARALYSIS

During the troubled era of the Roosevelt administration the president rallied the nation with his famous utterance, "We have nothing to fear but fear itself." President Franklin Delano Roosevelt understood that fear is a powerful force. It can paralyze people and hold them tightly in bondage.

Fear takes many forms. It may include a fear of bodily harm, a fear of failure, or a fear of success with the responsibilities and expectations that accompany it. We hear the expression, "I was frozen with fear." To be frozen with fear refers to the paralysis by which the normal flow of things is arrested as ice jams lock the normal flow of a river.

We are a phobic people. A recent study listed the top ten phobias of American people. The list included fear of death (thanatophobia), fear of heights (acrophobia), fear of narrowly confining spaces (claustrophobia), the fear of strangers (xenophobia), and several others. At the top of the list was the fear of public speaking. I can relate to that one. A hollow sinking feeling attacks the stomach. The hands become clammy. The throat muscles tense. It can become so severe that people "freeze" when they are called upon to speak. The memory fails. The mind goes blank. The mouth opens but no words come forth. Perhaps the root of this fear is simply the fear of saying or doing something foolish. Ironically, the fear itself produces just that effect.

No one wants to do something stupid in front of a crowd. The pressure in front of large groups can be tremendous. The athlete knows the dread of "choking" under such pressure. Recently a reporter interviewed a contestant in a golf tournament who was winning until the final holes. Suddenly the player's game fell apart and his score skyrocketed. In the press tent a reporter asked, "What happened out there?" The golfer replied simply, "I choked."

It was refreshing to hear this candid reply. The reporter was accustomed to hearing other explanations such as, "I lost my concentration," or "I was distracted by a camera shutter clicking," or "My ball took a strange bounce into a hazard." Normally professional athletes do not respond by saying, "I choked."

But even the most accomplished performers choke. They all know what it feels like. Fear comes over them in such a way as to grip their muscles in a vise. The smooth flow of the golf swing becomes stiff and jerky, with disastrous results.

What causes choking? The obvious answer is the fear of losing, of failing to achieve a much sought-after goal. The fear of being humiliated by playing badly may be the exact force that causes bad play.

But the fear may be more complex. Many athletes have a real fear of winning. If one wins he rises into a new status. A new level of expectation and its pressures is reached. Also, a person might actually feel guilty for winning, thinking that he does not deserve to be victorious.

Here there is an unspoken connection of fear with a nagging feeling of guilt. More about guilt in a moment.

FEAR OF CHANGE

For the moment, let us consider the factor of fearing a change in our status. We tend to be comfortable with the level of achievement we have attained. If we slip below that level, we experience a loss of confidence and self-esteem. That disturbs our comfort level. But if we rise above our normal achievement level, that is also discomforting. We are cast into strange and foreign waters. We are not sure what to expect. We are in a new zone of responsibility.

We have comfort zones in all sorts of areas. The comfort zone goes beyond sports. We have an economic comfort zone, an academic comfort zone, a social comfort zone, and so on. We also have a spiritual comfort zone. Too much change coming too quickly can be traumatic to the point of paralysis. We can handle change, but we don't wish to handle too much. And we also tend to become satisfied with the status quo. That can prevent the professional athlete—and the Christian—from striving too hard.

We speak of being "well-adjusted." What does that mean? To adjust is to respond to some kind of change in our lives. The child that moves from junior high school to high school must adjust. The single person who gets married must adjust. The businessman who gets a promotion must adjust. We admire people who can adapt creatively and productively to new situations. Perhaps we admire adaptation because we know how difficult it can be. Adjustments are not easy because they involve a change in our comfort zone.

Yet every Christian is called to change. We are commanded to move ahead in our spiritual progress. God is not inert, and He refuses to allow us to be. But with change comes the element of fear. Consider the example of Abraham:

Now the LORD *had said to Abram: "Get out of your country, from your kindred and from your father's house, to a land that I will show you. I will make you a great nation; I will bless you and make your name great; and you shall be a blessing. I will bless those who bless you, and I will curse him who curses you; and in you all the families of the earth shall be blessed."*

So Abram departed as the LORD *had spoken to him, and Lot went with him. And Abram was seventy-five years old when he departed from Haran. Genesis 12:1-4*

God called Abraham to move. He had to leave his comfort zone. He had to leave his town, his nation, and his family. He had to leave his roots, his security, and his familiar territory. He was ten years past the retirement age. He was an old dog who was expected to learn new tricks.

God's call to Abraham was a call to greatness. "I will make you a great nation" was the promise. The author of Hebrews commented later on Abraham's response to this fearful call:

*By faith Abraham obeyed when he was called to go out
to the place which he would afterward receive as an
inheritance. And he went out, not knowing where he
was going. By faith he sojourned in the land of promise
as in a foreign country, dwelling in tents with Isaac and
Jacob, the heirs with him of the same promise; for he
waited for the city which has foundations, whose
builder and maker is God. . . . Therefore from one
man, and him as good as dead, were born as many as
the stars of the sky in multitude—innumerable as the
sand which is by the seashore.*

*These all died in faith, not having received the
promises, but having seen them afar off were assured of
them, embraced them, and confessed that they were
strangers and pilgrims on the earth. Hebrews 11:8-13*

Abraham became a pilgrim. He was a man on the move
out of obedience to a divine call. The same may be said of
Moses, of Joshua, of David, of Paul, and especially of
Christ. They went where God told them to go. They did
what God told them to do, though that entailed a certain
lack of security. Likewise the Christian is called to forego a
feeling of security in this world—though the ultimate
security (the love of God) is a more than adequate com-
pensation for that.

THE LINKING OF FEAR AND GUILT
But how does this relate to guilt? As I mentioned, there is
often a close but subtle link between fear and guilt. Both
have a fierce power to paralyze. Both can make us halt—

or even retreat—in our spiritual journey. Both can keep us from reaching out to God. Both can distract us from the great goal of pleasing God.

Though we can distinguish between fear and guilt, we cannot always separate them. Frequently, paralyzing fear is a direct result of unresolved guilt. The ultimate fear is the fear of punishment at the hands of God. We are frightened by social rejection, parental disapproval, and peer judgment. We may be afraid of the sheriff or the IRS. But the most fearful thing is to fall into the hands of the living God. Though many people do not acknowledge it, they are afraid that their lives have angered the Creator of the universe. Consciousness of sin seems to be universal, and Christian and pagan alike know, or sense, that Almighty God is not pleased at our failings.

I once was invited by a psychiatrist to join him in his practice as a regular consultant. He was not particularly a religious man, but he said, "A great many of my patients need a priest more than they need a doctor. Many of them suffer from problems that at root are tied up with guilt."

To be a psychiatrist requires a lengthy term of academic study. A psychiatrist must first learn medicine and qualify as an M.D. before going on to his specialty. Yet with all his years of academic training he receives little or no education in theology.

Guilt is ultimately a theological problem. Without a thorough knowledge of theology, the psychiatrist is seriously hampered in dealing with guilt-ridden people. He cannot, unless he is a believer, understand that guilt is something very real, for real human beings do feel guilt over their acts and attitudes.

Sadly, so many people pay to have professional therapists listen to their woes, while the therapists may have little or no understanding of sin and guilt. Problems that appear to be mainly physiological may have deep roots in human guilt. Many marriage counselors counsel people who face problems of sexual dysfunction that threaten the marital union. Problems of so-called "frigidity" and "impotence" are *always* rooted in some form of guilt or fear. Assuming that the problem is merely a "mechanical failure" is very unfair to the patient.

God is loving and forgiving. God is also the Creator and Sustainer of the universe. He is a force to be reckoned with. Even people who have only rudimentary ideas about God seem to sense that God (even if they no longer use the word *God*) is a moral being who is disappointed at our troubled world. This powerful Being is intimidating for both pagan and believer. We remember Moses' and the Israelites' response to the presence of God at Sinai. So terrifying was it that the people could not endure His presence, and Moses himself was led to exclaim, "I am exceedingly afraid and trembling" (Hebrews 12:21).

Though modern man seems to do everything in his power to insulate himself from any thoughts about the terror of God, he is not able to erase such fears entirely from his conscience. The pagan still trembles at the rustling of a leaf; the wicked still flee when no man pursues. There remains a nagging, mostly unspoken fear, that

God is crouched, lying in wait for us, ready to pounce upon us at any moment. We are still afraid of things that go bump in the night.

Recently the elders of our local church went on a weekend retreat for fun and fellowship. They arrived at a country home on a Friday night. The event featured four-wheel-drive buggies that the elders revved up for a midnight frolic. There were not enough buggies to go around, so one enterprising elder joined the frolic by climbing aboard a riding lawn mower. He drove slowly into the night to join the others. Suddenly he let out a scream of fear. He saw the shadow of something looming up behind him and felt the ominous touch of some foreign object against his neck. Then he screamed. As his friends rushed to his aid they fell over laughing at the sight of their friend frozen in terror. He was firmly in the grasp of the grass-catcher attachment that had risen in the night to attack him. Perhaps our eternal fear of the dark is at root the fear of God, a God who will (we fear) eventually cause our sins to catch up with us.

No one dares turn his back on God. We know that He sees our every move, that He notes our every thought. The fear of punishment at His hands can never be eradicated by those stricken with guilt.

In considering guilt we must be careful to distinguish between guilt and guilt *feelings*. Guilt feelings are subjective. They arise from within us. We can feel guilty even when there is no guilt. Guilt, however, is objective. It involves a real state of affairs. Whenever we sin we incur guilt. Guilt involves a debtor relationship to God. It is tied to sin.

The Westminster Catechism defines sin as "Any want of conformity to, or transgression of the Law of God." This is a masterful definition. It captures both sins of omission and sins of commission. When we fail to conform to the Law of God, we fall short of what God requires. We do not do what God commands. That is a sin of omission. When we transgress the Law of God, we do what God forbids. This is a sin of commission.

FACING REAL GUILT

Either way, by omission or commission, if we violate the Law of God we incur guilt. That guilt is real and objective. It is also devastating. Appropriate guilt feelings may or may not accompany guilt. We know that guilt feelings make us uncomfortable. We employ numerous devices to rid ourselves of those feelings. We excuse ourselves. We rationalize. We shift the blame to other people or to our circumstances. We blame society. We blame our environment. We blame our parents. We appeal to everything we can to escape the pain of personal responsibility. We use every kind of avoidance mechanism, because our guilt is indeed great. It is too much to handle, and unless we cope with it in the right way—appealing to the saving work of Christ—we spend valuable time and energy in running from guilt.

We have learned how to harden our hearts. We can lose

the capacity to blush. Jeremiah declared the word of God to Judah: "You have had a harlot's forehead; you refuse to be ashamed" (Jeremiah 3:3).

Here we see the refusal to repent linked to the squashing of guilt feelings. The people of Judah protested their innocence while they continuously violated the Law of God. By repeated sin they acquired the forehead of a harlot. That is, they forgot how to be ashamed.

But the lack of guilt feelings does not excuse real guilt. A man on trial for murder would find his defense flimsy indeed if all he said was, "But I don't feel guilty." There are psychopathic killers who feel no remorse for their crimes. The lack of remorse, however, does not excuse their deeds.

A sad commentary on contemporary life is the frequency with which counselors seek to relieve people's guilt problems by focusing on the removal of guilt feelings. To relieve guilt, people are told that they are victims of their environment and of the oppressive moral standards of outmoded religion. This applies not only to non-Christians, but to Christians as well. Many Christians, living with a burdensome guilt over past or present sins, tell their woes to therapists who say, in effect, "Considering the life you've had to lead, no wonder you've behaved in this way. As long as you understand that, there is no real problem." But it isn't true, is it? Explaining the problem does not eliminate the problem. Guilt only disappears when we are made right with God. That rightness is available at any time, for we serve a forgiving God. But He does not force His children to ask His forgiveness. They do so willingly, or they torment themselves with guilt that the therapists cannot explain away.

I was approached by a distressed college girl who was engaged to be married. She explained that she had been sexually involved with her fiancé and was feeling guilty about it. She related to me that she had gone to her school counselor who told her, "The reason you feel guilty is because you have been a victim of a Victorian ethic or a Puritan taboo. You need to understand that your behavior is perfectly normal. It is a healthy part of mature self-expression and of preparation for marriage."

The girl then said to me, "But Professor Sproul, I still feel guilty!" I said, "Perhaps the reason you feel guilty is because you *are* guilty. The prohibition for fornication was not invented by Queen Victoria, nor was it the creation of the Puritans. It is God who forbids fornication. When we break the laws of God we incur real guilt. The only remedy I know for real guilt is real forgiveness."

I explained to the young woman that the price tag for real forgiveness is real repentance. Real repentance is what the individual must do himself. No one else can repent for me. I cannot repent for anyone else. I encouraged the woman to get alone with God, to go before Him on her knees. Without me. Without the counselors. Then I promised her—indeed, I guaranteed her—that in God's sight her guilt would be removed and that she would once again be a virgin in God's sight. Then she would be free of the fear and paralysis that come in the wake of guilt.

As Christians we must examine our lives. We must ask ourselves two basic questions: At what point am I paralyzed in my spiritual growth? Why am I paralyzed?

Chances are that if we can answer these two questions accurately, we can identify those areas of fear and guilt that are in need of resolution. The grace of God—especially the grace of forgiveness—is the most potent force available to us to be freed from paralysis.

God does not want us paralyzed. He wants us to feel so secure in Him that we need have no real fear of the world and its obstacles. He wishes us to be conscious of our sins, but He takes no joy in our being immobilized by guilt. God is, like any good human parent, eager to lead us out of a life of fear and guilt so that we are free to do what is right and pleasing. What freedom is offered to us! Freedom *from* guilt, freedom *from* fear, freedom *to* serve and please God with everything we are. No therapist in the world can offer us such a life.

CHAPTER NINE

REAL
FORGIVENESS

We have seen the paralyzing force of unresolved guilt. The reality of guilt is a cumbersome burden for anyone to carry about with him. We remember the dreadful weight that the hero of *The Pilgrim's Progress* dragged through his travels. We remember the awful "body of death" of which the apostle Paul spoke. Those who saw the Hollywood movie *The Mission* recall the graphic torture the penitent mercenary soldier bore as he climbed a mountain weighted down with a bundle of armor.

To cast off this burden is to know the sweetness of relief. To hear what Isaiah heard—"Your sins are forgiven"—is to hear the music of freedom. For centuries Roman Catholics have experienced a moment of relief in the confessional as the priest pronounced the words, *Te Absolvo*—"I forgive you."

In Roman Catholicism, confession belongs to the sacrament of penance. This sacrament was repudiated by the vast majority of Protestant churches during the Reformation. As a result, many Protestants look at the Roman Catholic practice of confession with a jaundiced eye. We hear the continuing protest expressed in words like, "Why should I confess my sins to a priest? Christ is the High Priest. I can confess my sins to Him directly. I don't need an earthly priest!" Is this realistic, or are we just justifying an anti-Catholic prejudice?

It is a sad fact of church history that most Protestants

do not know what it is they are protesting. The passing of time has dimmed the classic point of protest. What is left is a somewhat ambiguous prejudice against Rome that focuses on trivial matters.

PENANCE AND PROTESTANTISM

To put the debate in perspective, let us look briefly at the historical issues that provoked the Reformers. The Reformation was triggered by an abuse centering on the sacrament of penance. Penance was seen by Rome as a necessary step for restoring saving grace to those who had committed a mortal sin. Rome calls the sacrament of penance the "second plank of justification for those who have made shipwreck of their souls."

Why the "second plank of justification"? In Roman theology the first plank of justification is found in the sacrament of baptism. By baptism justifying grace is infused into the human soul. A baptized person remains in a state of grace until or unless that person commits a mortal sin. A mortal sin is called "mortal" because it kills or destroys saving grace. A person who commits a mortal sin is in need of being justified again. The new justification comes through the sacrament of penance.

The sacrament of penance has several parts to it. It includes confession, contrition, priestly absolution, and works of satisfaction. The Roman Catholic church defines penance not so much as a feeling as an activity. It is something a person *does*. Traditional biblical texts that Protestant Bibles translate *repent* are translated by the words "do penance" in Catholic versions of Scripture.

The Reformation controversy centered on one aspect of penance, the aspect of *works of satisfaction*. In modern terms it works like this. A person comes to the privacy of the confessional and tells the priest his sins. The person prays the prayer of confession and awaits the priest's words of absolution. Then the priest prescribes a penance to perform. The penitent may be required to say so many "Hail Marys" or "Our Fathers" or other ritual prayers. At times more rigorous and demanding penalties are required. These are the works of satisfaction. They "satisfy" the demands of God and make it fitting or "congruous" for God to restore justification to the penitent.

During the Middle Ages the act of almsgiving was seen as a legitimate form of doing penance. The church was very careful to point out that salvation was not for sale. One cannot "purchase" forgiveness by giving money to the poor or to the church. Yet almsgiving motivated by a genuine spirit of repentance and love for God was a fitting work of satisfaction.

A serious problem with this erupted in the sixteenth century. Rome was involved in a massive building program with the construction of St. Peter's Basilica. The church authorized papal indulgences for sins for those who made contributions to the project out of sincere and godly motives. (An indulgence was remission of temporal or purgatorial punishment for sins committed.)

In Germany, William Tetzel, an unscrupulous representative of Rome began to sell indulgences, particularly to uneducated peasants, as if these indulgences could be received without the proper attitude. In other words, for paying a fee a person could receive remission for sins. There was no need for genuine repentance nor for penitential acts of charity. The chief salesman, the monk Tetzel, provoked the wrath of Martin Luther for cheapening the system of penance. The famous Ninety-five Theses were posted in response to these abuses.

The indulgence controversy opened Pandora's box. The debate led to a full-scale issue of the whole question of justification. Ultimately Luther declared the doctrine of justification by faith alone. He attacked the sacrament of penance at the point of works of satisfaction.

Luther argued that the total satisfaction offered for our sins was performed by Christ. No person can add to that satisfaction. No human can supplement the merit of Jesus by any form of human merit, including the so-called "congruous merit" *(meritum de congruo)* that can be gained by works of satisfaction. Justifying grace is offered freely to all who genuinely confess their sins and embrace Christ by faith.

Luther considered other issues as "trifles" compared with the central issue of justification by faith alone. He called justification by faith alone "the article upon which the individual believer stands or falls."

As a result, most Protestant Christians no longer have a confessional. We almost never hear from human beings the audible words *Te Absolvo*.

Protestants are often rankled by the idea of a human priest saying, "I forgive you." In Rome's defense we must point out that by no means does the church intend to declare that a priest has the intrinsic right to forgive sins. In Rome's view the priest is carrying out the authority Jesus gave to His apostles when He said, "If you forgive the sins of any, they are forgiven them" (John 20:23). This is not far removed from what Protestant ministers do when they declare the "Assurance of Pardon" from the pulpit on Sunday morning.

THE BURNING NEED FOR ASSURANCE

Sadly, many Protestants do not feel an assurance of forgiveness for their sins. They are plagued by persistent guilt feelings. We live as if the Cross never happened. We harbor a lingering, nagging feeling that somehow the Atonement of Jesus is not enough to cover our sins. Grace is something other people need. We want to atone for our own sins. We think that we must somehow make up for our guilt.

I once spoke with a woman who said to me, "How can I receive forgiveness for my sins? I have prayed and prayed to God for forgiveness for my sins, but I still feel guilty."

The woman was seeking theological advice. She looked at me as if she expected me to come up with some secret, esoteric device to grant her full assurance of her forgiveness. I replied, "I think you need to pray for forgiveness one more time."

My answer not only disappointed her; it clearly annoyed her. She said, "Didn't you hear what I said? I've prayed repeatedly. What good will praying one more time do?"

I answered, "This time I want you to ask God to forgive you for your arrogance."

Now she was really angry. "Arrogance! What do you mean arrogance? I've humbled myself time and again in prayer. Why is that arrogance?"

I explained that God has declared that if we confess our sins to Him He will forgive us of our sins: "If we confess our sins, He is faithful and just to forgive us our sins and to cleanse us from all unrighteousness" (1 John 1:9).

Just as there is a crucial difference between guilt and guilt feelings, so there is a similar difference between forgiveness and feelings of forgiveness. Guilt is objective; guilt feelings are subjective. Forgiveness is objective; feelings of forgiveness are subjective.

If God declares a person forgiven, that person is truly, objectively, really and fully forgiven. Forgiveness is now a reality. If the warm feelings of peace of mind flow out of the reality of forgiveness, that is a sweet and wonderful bonus. But it is not the final test of forgiveness.

This is a two-edged sword. A person can manufacture feelings of forgiveness when they are not forgiven. I've heard numerous people tell me that God has given them "peace" about doing things God clearly forbids. I've heard people say that God gave them peace of mind to commit adultery. Such statements must certainly grieve the Spirit.

God gives forgiveness freely to the repentant. But He never grants license for sin. He is not the author of peace to the impenitent. That peace is a false peace, a lying peace.

I asked the woman to pray for forgiveness for her arrogance for this reason: God has promised to forgive our sins if we truly repent and turn to Him in confession. God's promises are faithful. It is arrogant for us to refuse to forgive anyone whom God forgives, including ourselves. Consider the words of Paul: "Who are you to judge another's servant? To his own master he stands or falls. Indeed, he shall be made to stand, for God is able to make him stand" (Romans 14:4).

Here the apostle warns against judging other people whom Christ has received. If we are not permitted to judge others whom God has forgiven, how much less are we permitted to judge ourselves when God has forgiven us?

When God forgives a person, that person is forgiven whether we feel the forgiveness or not. The sensuous Christian lives by his feelings. The spiritual Christian lives by the Word of God. If God declares that I am forgiven, then it is sheer arrogance for me to refuse to forgive myself.

Perhaps the woman I was counseling did not feel forgiven because she doubted the truthfulness of God's promise. Perhaps it was something else. Perhaps she was reacting against grace. Again, grace is all right for other people, but she was too proud to accept it for herself. She wanted to *earn* her forgiveness. She did justification the old-fashioned way, the Smith-Barney method: she wanted to *earn* it.

Jesus told a short parable that is easy for us to understand with our minds but is difficult for us to get in our bloodstream:

And which of you, having a servant plowing or tending sheep, will say to him when he has come in from the field, "Come at once and sit down to eat"? But will he not rather say to him, "Prepare something for my supper, and gird yourself and serve me till I have eaten and drunk, and afterward you will eat and drink"? Does he thank that servant because he did the things that were commanded him? I think not. So likewise you, when you have done all those things which you are commanded, say, "We are unprofitable servants. We have done what was our duty to do." Luke 17:7-10.

We are unprofitable servants. If we did every single thing that God has commanded us to do, we would have nothing of which to boast. Perfect obedience to Him is our duty. We have no claim to extra merit.

The fact is, we have not done everything He has commanded us to do. So how can we possibly make it up? If we did everything we were commanded and were still unprofitable servants, how could we possibly be profitable in our shortcomings? We simply cannot. That is why grace is absolutely necessary for all of us.

We are debtors who cannot pay our debts. We are like the unjust steward who when he was called into account cried out within himself, "What shall I do? For my master is taking the stewardship away from me. I cannot dig; I am ashamed to beg" (Luke 16:3).

That is our dilemma. We cannot dig and we are

ashamed to beg. But beg we must. That is all a debtor who cannot pay can do.

We live by grace. We walk by forgiveness. We rejoice in the certainty that when we confess our sins God promises to forgive them.

FORGIVING AND FORGETTING

The Bible tells us that when God forgives us, He removes our sins from us as far as the east is from the west:

He has not dealt with us according to our sins, nor punished us according to our iniquities. For as the heavens are high above the earth, so great is His mercy toward them who fear Him. As far as the east is from the west, so far has He removed our transgressions from us. Psalm 103:10-12

When God forgives us of our sins He casts them into the Sea of Forgetfulness. Jeremiah declares the promise: "For I will forgive their iniquity, and their sin I will remember no more" (Jeremiah 31:34). What does the Bible mean when it says that God will no longer remember our sins? In what way does God forgive and forget? We must be careful to note that these expressions use human figures of speech as a manner of speaking. We must not jump to the conclusion that the Almighty, Omniscient, Immutable God suddenly has a lapse in His memory. God knows everything about my life. He is very much aware of every sin I have ever committed. When He blots out my transgression, it is not that he actually loses all knowledge of it. Rather He blots it out of the record book. He treats me as if I had not sinned. He covers my sin with the righteousness of Christ.

The forgetting of God is a relational forgetting. That is, He remembers it no more *against* me. When God forgives me of my sin He doesn't hold it against me. He bears no grudges. He harbors no lingering hostility. My relationship with Him is totally and completely restored. He does for me what He promised in the book of Isaiah: " 'Come now, and let us reason together,' says the LORD: 'Though your sins are like scarlet, they shall be as white as snow; though they are red like crimson, they shall be as wool' " (Isaiah 1:18).

FORGIVING OTHER PEOPLE

One of the most terrifying elements of the Lord's Prayer is the petition "Forgive us our debts, as we forgive our debtors" (Matthew 6:12). We tend to be far more ungenerous in forgiving others than God is in forgiving us. If God were to be as reluctant to forgive us as we are in forgiving those who sin against us, we would be in serious trouble.

As Christians we are forgiven people. We are likewise called to be forgiving people. The key to forgiving others is found in Jesus' teaching:

Take heed to yourselves. If your brother sins against you, rebuke him; and if he repents, forgive him. And if he sins against you seven times in a day, and seven times

in a day returns to you, saying, "I repent," you shall
forgive him. And the apostles said to the Lord, "Increase
our faith." Luke 17:3-5

Much confusion exists about the Christian's responsibility to forgive others. Two major issues need clarification. They are: Whom are we required to forgive? What does forgiveness entail?

On the question of whom we must forgive, there is a widespread misunderstanding in Christian circles. Somehow, somewhere, the idea gained currency that Christians are under obligation to grant unqualified, unilateral forgiveness to anyone who sins against them. For example, if a person attacks my character unjustly, it is assumed that I must simply absorb the grievance and forgive that person immediately.

Where did such an idea originate? Perhaps a clue may be found in the example of Jesus as well as in some of His teaching. We see Jesus praying for the forgiveness of His executioners while He was on the cross. "Father, forgive them for they do not know what they do" (Luke 23:34). We hear Jesus teach in the Sermon on the Mount, "Blessed are the merciful: for they shall obtain mercy" (Matthew 5:7). Again He declares, "But I tell you not to resist an evil person. But whoever slaps you on your right cheek, turn the other to him also" (Matthew 5:39).

Jesus clearly sets forth an ethic of charity. We are called to be forbearing, patient, and long-suffering toward those who abuse us. Jesus commands us to be willing to go the second mile. A spirit of contentiousness, bitterness, argumentativeness and belligerence has no place in the kingdom of God.

When Jesus tells us to "turn the other cheek," He is using a Jewish idiom that involves bearing insults. We notice in the text that Jesus said that if someone smites us on the *right* cheek we are to turn the other cheek. This is usually understood to mean that if someone hits us on one side of the face we should offer the other side as well. The saying seems to teach that we have no right to self-defense if we are physically attacked. We must be doormats to anyone who wants to beat up on us.

How far do we take this? Does the text imply that if someone kidnaps our daughter we should offer the kidnapper our son as well? I think not. Think about the words Jesus uses. He speaks of hitting on the *right cheek*. Suppose you are standing in front of someone, face to face, and that person wants to hit you on your right cheek. How can that be accomplished? It can be done one of two ways. Either the person must strike you with his left hand or the person must hit you with the *back* of his right hand. The vast majority of people are right-handed. A right-handed person does not normally attack with the left hand (unless they have a highly trained left hook).

In Jewish idiom, to be struck on the right cheek has reference to an insulting slap of the back of the right hand. In the Middle Ages it was the sign of a challenge to a duel. A person might take off his glove and hit you with the glove by a backhanded slap. It is the ancient idiom of the insult. In all probability Jesus' hearers understood Him to mean that if a person insults you, you are not to respond in kind. We are not to return evil for evil. The central focus is on peaceful restraint and nonviolent responses to verbal abuse. During His trial Jesus was mocked and slapped, and though He could have called on legions of angels to assist Him, He chose to bear the insults in silence. He blessed those who cursed Him and did good to them who hated Him. In a word, He showed love toward His enemies.

HOW FAR TO FORGIVE

Yet all of this does not nullify the fact that biblical law has manifold provision for the seeking of justice in the case of wrongful injury. Virtually every Christian church has some provision to deal with grievances within the church by the valid use of church courts. There are also provisions for the use of civil courts to settle serious disputes.

Our preliminary conclusion is this: If we are sinned against we *may* exercise unilateral forgiveness, but it is not an absolute obligation in every circumstance. Here we see the crucial distinction between *may* and *must*. We notice in Jesus' extended teaching on forgiveness in Luke 17 that He says, "If your brother sins against you, rebuke him: and if he repents, forgive him." Here the one who sins is a brother. It is possible that this mandate does not apply to everyone who sins against us. We are to treat all people as *neighbors*, but not everyone is a *brother*. A brother has specific reference to a fellow Christian.

At least in the case of being sinned against by a fellow

Christian we have specific instructions. The first is to *rebuke* the brother. We are not thereby commanded to bear all sins in silence. Jesus gives clear expression to rebuke or admonish the guilty party. What follows is of central importance. Jesus says, "And if he repents, forgive him." Here we see a conditional clause, "if he repents." Presumably if the brother does not repent we are under no obligation to grant unilateral forgiveness. Just as God requires repentance from us before He grants forgiveness, we may exact the same requirement.

Of course we *may* choose to forgive someone who does not repent, but that is not the same thing as saying that we *must* forgive the impenitent person. However, if the condition of repentance is met, then we are under obligation to grant forgiveness. If the brother repents then we *must* forgive him. Refusal to forgive a repentant person is itself a sin that requires forgiveness.

When I was in seminary I was a student minister in a small church. I insulted the daughter of a woman who was a pillar of the church. The daughter was deeply offended. I went to her and apologized profusely. She refused to forgive me. I went two more times and apologized literally in tears. Still she refused to forgive me.

It came time for my monthly meeting with the minister who was appointed moderator of our session. He was my pastoral supervisor. He was an eighty-five-year-old retired missionary who had spent fifty years in the interior of China, five years of that in a communist prison camp. He was a man of extraordinary godliness. I went to him with deep embarrassment for the mess I had made of my first pastoral experience. I told him what I had done. He listened carefully and then replied calmly, "Young man, you have made two serious mistakes. The first is obvious. You should not have insulted the daughter. The second mistake is this: You should not have apologized three times. After the first apology the ball was in her court. If she refused to forgive you she is heaping coals of fire upon her own head."

There was wisdom in the old saint's words. If we sin against a person, we must repent, and then it is over for us. Likewise, if our brother repents of a sin against us, we must forgive. But that leads us to the next important consideration. What does forgiveness involve?

We have already seen that when God forgives us He no longer holds our sin against us. He forgets it insofar as He remembers it no more against us. This, however, does not preclude restitution. Restitution is not the same thing as works of satisfaction in the Roman Catholic sacrament of penance. Restitution means paying what we owe.

For example, if I steal money from my employer and then repent of my theft, it is not enough for me simply to confess my sin and apologize. I must also return the money and pay whatever penalties are involved. Zacchaeus understood this principle of restitution when he declared to Jesus: "Look, Lord, I give half of my goods to the poor; and if I have taken anything from anyone by false accusation, I restore fourfold" (Luke 19:8).

When I repent I must still pay what I owe. It means being willing to accept the consequences of my actions and attending penalties. We distinguish between earthly or temporal guilt and heavenly or eternal guilt. If I break the earthly law and ask God to forgive me, I may receive His eternal pardon but still face the penalties of my temporal guilt.

The old Hollywood gangster movies often portrayed execution scenes in which a convict walked the "last mile" to the gallows or the electric chair in the company of a priest who was intoning prayers for forgiveness. The image of the noose side by side with the Bible seemed radically inconsistent.

Yet the Bible calls for real penalties to be enacted against lawbreakers, even against penitent, confessing lawbreakers. The civil magistrate may temper justice with mercy, but he is not required by God to waive all penalties in the case of a penitent criminal. The repentant person pleases God with his contriteness, but society has a right to demand that justice be done.

FORGIVENESS AND REPEATED SINS

How does forgiveness apply to situations where the marriage vows have been broken? Let us suppose that a man commits adultery and his sin is discovered. He confesses his guilt, indicates deep shame and remorse and asks his wife to forgive him. What is the wife's moral duty in such a circumstance?

The question has both a simple answer and a complex one. First the simple answer. Jesus requires us to forgive those who sin against us who repent of their sin. Therefore, the wife *must* forgive her penitent husband.

The complex question is this: What does such forgiveness entail? A related question is this: May the wife forgive her husband and still divorce him?

On the surface it may seem absurd to even ask such a question. It would seem that forgiveness would exclude any thought of divorce. But it is not that simple. There are basically three approaches taken to the question of divorce in the case of the penitent adulterer.

Approach 1: There are many Christians who are persuaded that divorce is never justifiable on any grounds whatsoever. For this group the solution is easy. The wife may not divorce her husband even if he is not repentant.

Approach 2: This approach allows for divorce on the grounds of adultery. It takes the position that if the man is unrepentant the wife may justly divorce him. But if the man repents, then it is the duty of the wife to forgive him and stay married to him.

Approach 3: This view also recognizes the right of divorce in the case of adultery. It does not demand divorce in the case of adultery but permits it. Here the view is that even if the husband repents, the wife may justly exercise her right of divorce. She must forgive her husband and must receive him as a brother in Christ. But she is not required to stay married to him. The forfeiture of marital rights are seen as part of the civil penalties that may be invoked in the crime.

Although such issues are exceedingly difficult to resolve, one thing is clear: Forgiveness does not necessarily mean that no penalties or restitution follow. By forgiveness is meant a maintaining of a personal relationship without estrangement. It also means that the sin is not rehashed in the personal relationship.

In Luke 17 Jesus says that if your brother trespasses against you seven times in a day and repents seven times in a day—"You shall forgive him."

Jesus does not allow for "three strikes and you're out." If my brother sins against me, repents, is forgiven, and then does exactly the same thing, I may not say to him, "That's two!"

I may not keep a scorecard of offenses. If I forgive the first transgression and put it aside by forgiving my brother, I am promising to hold it against him no longer. If he sins again I must say, "That's one!" because the first sin has no bearing on the second.

Now that is a tall order. It is particularly in the realm of repeated sins that we find the greatest difficulty in being merciful. We have a saying—"Fool me once, shame on you. Fool me twice, shame on me."

To forgive the same offense twice is exceedingly difficult. To forgive seven times pushes our ability to be gracious to the extreme. It is no wonder that the disciples responded to Jesus' command by saying, "Increase our faith" (Luke 17:5).

FORGIVENESS FOR FORMER SINS

Can a Christian be forgiven for sins committed before conversion? The obvious answer is yes. If the answer were no, we would still be under the curse of God's judgment. But the Atonement of Christ is made for all of our sins.

The answer to the next question will not find such widespread agreement. Is a Christian responsible for sins committed prior to conversion? Again, on the surface it would appear that the obvious answer to the question is yes. The whole principle of restitution would apply.

Those who answer no usually do so in a particular context based on a particular argument. Again, the context is marriage and divorce. Suppose a man divorces his wife illegitimately, that is, without biblical grounds. Five years later he is converted to Christ. He falls in love with a Christian woman and wants to marry her. How does the church respond? Is the man required to seek reconciliation with his former wife or may he move freely into a new marriage?

Those who argue that the man is free to move into a new marriage without any obligation to his former wife often argue this point on the grounds that the man is a "new creature" in Christ. Being born anew, the man has no responsibility for what he did before conversion because the man was not the same man then.

This is a woeful distortion of biblical principle. Though indeed I am a new creation in Christ, it is "I," R. C. Sproul, who is a new creation. R. C. Sproul may be born again, but there is a personal continuity between the new R. C. Sproul and the old R. C. Sproul. The new R. C. Sproul is still required to pay the old R. C. Sproul's debts.

Imagine this scenario. At four o'clock in the afternoon,

Mr. Smith robs his employer of ten thousand dollars. At five o'clock in the afternoon Mr. Smith is converted to Christ. May he now keep the money? On the contrary. Far from conversion eliminating a person's obligations, it actually increases them. A reborn man should be all the more scrupulous in his willingness to pay his debts and make full restitution wherever possible.

Full restitution is an integral part of full repentance. It is the mark of true repentance. True repentance is necessary for true forgiveness. If our goal is full and complete forgiveness, we must be willing to offer full and complete repentance. If our goal is to please God, we must repent. We may see the price tag as high. In fact, here we find the real meaning of "cheap grace." The value of full forgiveness is infinite. Compared to the benefits we receive in full forgiveness, the price tag of repentance is outrageously cheap. There is no greater bargain to be found in this world than the bargain of forgiving grace.

The forgiving God we serve is pleased when we gratefully accept His forgiveness. He is also pleased when we are willing to act as adults and make amends for the sins we have committed against others. If we read the New Testament correctly, it seems the kingdom of God is composed of responsible and forgiven people.

CHAPTER TEN
THE CARNAL CHRISTIAN

We have seen that guilt and fear are dreadful burdens to carry through life. The sweetness of the gospel is found in these words: "Behold, this has touched your lips; your iniquity is taken away, and your sin purged" (Isaiah 6:7). The hot coal touching the stricken Isaiah's lips symbolized the power of the forgiving God to raise up a guilt-ridden soul.

When God removes our iniquity, when He takes away our iniquity from us, we experience a liberation unlike anything the world can match. No windfall profit, no military victory, no election results, no romance or job promotion can liberate the spirit of man as much as one sentence from God: "Your sins are forgiven."

The apostle Paul once used a vivid and almost crude word picture to describe the awful burden of guilt: "O wretched man that I am! Who will deliver me from this body of death?" (Romans 7:24).

I say that this word picture borders upon crudeness because of the source of the phrase "body of death." There was a tradition in many ancient cultures whereby a person guilty of cold-blooded murder was forced to go about chained to the body of his victim. Imagine being bound to a decaying corpse. Having to drag a dead body around while it underwent the process of putrefaction was enough to drive men mad.

It is a fitting analogy of the Christian life. Our old nature is crucified with Christ. The old man is under a death sentence. We are to reckon it already dead in Christ. The Christian is a new creation, made alive by the Holy Spirit.

But herein is our dilemma. The old man may be declared dead, but we are not altogether free of him. We still carry around that old nature of wretchedness with us. It is as though that corpse does not know that it has died.

I once explained the dilemma like this: Our old nature is like a chicken with its head cut off. It runs wildly around the barnyard, flapping its wings and squawking all over the place. My image worked well until a farmer politely reminded me that once a chicken's head is cut off it no longer has the capacity to squawk!

Chickens without heads may not squawk, but our old nature squawks like mad. It creates a ruckus like no dead thing should be able to do. In a word, the old man continues to incite us to sin. That is why the Christian life requires daily trips to the throne of grace for a fresh and vital experience of forgiveness.

It is a source of irritation for me to hear preachers proclaim, "Come to Jesus, and all your problems will be over!" It is a zealous proclamation of the gospel that simply is not true. In one sense life doesn't begin to get complicated until one becomes a Christian. When we are born of the Spirit we are born anew into a fierce struggle between the old man and the new man. It is the struggle a person faces when they have a renewed and sensitized conscience.

The old life was one of consistent disobedience. It is the life Paul described to the Ephesians:

*And you He made alive, who were dead in trespasses
and sins, in which you once walked according to the
course of this world, according to the prince of the
power of the air, the spirit who now works in the sons
of disobedience, among whom also we all once
conducted ourselves in the lusts of our flesh, fulfilling
the desires of the flesh and of the mind, and were by
nature children of wrath, just as the others. Ephesians
2:1-3*

This passage shows the consistent pattern of disobedience that characterizes the unregenerate life. Life has one course, the course of this world. It has one master, Satan, the prince of the power of the air. Augustine once declared that a man is like a horse. The horse is either ridden by Satan or by the Spirit of God. The image is helpful except for one thing. In the Christian life we are not as consistent as we were when we were ridden by Satan alone. To be sure, Satan has been thrown off our backs and the Spirit is now in the saddle. But Satan still does everything in his power to clutch at the reins. The horse still veers from side to side. He rears up and bucks, trying to throw the new master from the saddle. We are still whinnying in rebellion, seeking to have our noses stroked by our old master.

Paul put it this way:

*For we know that the law is spiritual, but I am carnal,
sold under sin. For what I am doing, I do not
understand. For what I will to do, that I do not
practice; but what I hate, that I do. If, then, I do what I
will not to do, I agree with the law that it is good. But
now, it is no longer I who do it, but sin that dwells in*

me. For I know that in me (that is, in my flesh)
nothing good dwells; for to will is present with me, but
how to perform what is good I do not find. For the
good that I will to do, I do not do; but the evil I will
not to do, that I practice. Romans 7:14-19

THE ANTINOMIAN VIEW

Romans 7 is the subject of much controversy. The first
concerns the concept of the so-called carnal Christian.
There is a widespread notion within evangelical Christianity that there are two distinctive types of Christians.
There is the carnal Christian and the spiritual Christian.
The carnal Christian is a believer who does not have
Christ on the throne of his life and thereby lives a pattern
of constant disobedience. Then there is the "Spirit-filled"
Christian whose life is characterized by a life of obedience
and spiritual devotion. Here Christ reigns on the throne of
the Christian life.

This distinction is fraught with peril. The peril has two
faces, both of which are ugly distortions of the truth. The
first distortion is that of the ancient heresy of antinomianism. Antinomianism means literally "anti-lawism." The
song of the antinomian is this: "Free from the law, O
blessed condition; I can sin all I want and still have remission!" This distortion rests upon a false view of grace and
forgiveness. It includes the idea that a person can receive
Christ as Savior but not as Lord. It assumes a faith without obedience, a faith with no fruit of good works. This is
precisely the kind of "dead faith" of which James writes, a

faith that is no faith, a faith that can never please God.

Here the carnal Christian is one who is said to believe in Christ but lives a life of consistent carnality, giving no evidence of the fruit of the Spirit. This represents a fatal contradiction in terms. Such a person may not be called a carnal Christian. He must be considered a carnal non-Christian. If a person manifests a life of pure and consistent carnality, he is no Christian. He has not the Spirit of Christ living in him. It is a flat impossibility to be born of the Spirit and have no change in one's life. A Christian with no fruit is simply not a Christian. Antinomianism is the spirit of lawlessness that reigns in the children of disobedience. The "faith" of a carnal Christian is no faith. It cannot justify the ungodly. It cannot be pleasing to God.

We remember that justification by faith alone is not by a faith that is alone. The central affirmation of all Protestantism is that we are justified by faith and not by works. But the instant that true justifying faith is present in the life of the believer, the person begins to change. That change will be evidenced in a life that moves to obedience. Good works necessarily flow out of true faith. The works do not justify us. It is the righteousness of Christ that justifies us. But if the works do not follow, it is proof positive that we do not have genuine faith and are therefore still unjustified people.

In the antinomian sense there is no such thing as a carnal Christian. The concept is as perilous as it is self-contradictory. The peril is this: People begin to think that all that is required to be saved is a *profession* of faith. But the Bible warns us that people can honor Christ with their lips while their hearts are far from Him. They can say they have faith without having what they claim to have: "What does it profit, my brethren, if someone says he has faith but does not have works? Can faith save him?" (James 2:14).

James answers his own question by declaring emphatically that such a faith is dead and can save no one.

We conclude then that although we are required to profess our faith, the mere profession of faith is not enough to save us. We must possess what we profess. It is the *possession* of saving faith that justifies us, not the mere *profession* of it.

THE PERFECTIONIST VIEW

The second ancient heresy of the distinction between two types of Christians, carnal and Spirit-filled, is the heresy of perfectionism. Here the error is in the opposite direction from antinomianism. Perfectionism teaches that there is a class of Christians who achieve moral perfection in this life. To be sure, credit is given to the Holy Spirit as the agent who brings total victory over sin to the Christian. But there is a kind of elitism in perfectionism, a feeling that those who have achieved perfection are somehow greater than other Christians. The "perfect" ones do not—officially—take credit for their state, but smugness and pride have a way of creeping in.

The peril of perfectionism is that it seriously distorts the human mind. Imagine the contortions through which we must put ourselves to delude us into thinking that we have in fact achieved a state of sinlessness.

Inevitably the error of perfectionism breeds one, or usually two, deadly delusions. To convince ourselves that we have achieved sinlessness, we must either suffer from a radical overestimation of our moral performance or we must seriously underestimate the requirements of God's law. The irony of perfectionism is this: Though it seeks to distance itself from antinomianism, it relentlessly and inevitably comes full circle to the same error.

To believe that we are sinless we must annul the standards of God's Law. We must reduce the level of divine righteousness to the level of our own performance. We must lie to ourselves both about the Law of God and about our own obedience. To do that requires that we quench the Spirit when He seeks to convict us of sin. Persons who do that are not so much Spirit-filled as they are Spirit-quenchers.

One of the true marks of our ongoing sanctification is the growing awareness of how far short we fall of reaching perfection. Perfectionism is really antiperfectionism in disguise. If we think we are becoming perfect, then we are far from becoming perfect.

I once encountered a young man who had been a Christian for about a year. He boldly declared to me that he had received the "second blessing" and was now enjoying a life of victory, a life of sinless perfection. I immediately turned his attention to Paul's teaching on Romans 7. Romans 7 is the biblical death blow to every doctrine of perfectionism. My young friend quickly replied with the classic agreement of the perfectionist heresy, namely, that in Romans 7 Paul is describing his former unconverted state.

I explained to the young man that it is exegetically impossible to dismiss Romans 7 as the expression of Paul's former life. We examined the passage closely and the man finally agreed that indeed Paul was writing in the present tense. His next response was, "Well, maybe Paul was speaking of his present experience, but he just hadn't received the second blessing yet."

I had a difficult time concealing my astonishment at this spiritual arrogance. I asked him pointedly, "You mean that you, at age nineteen, after one year of Christian faith, have achieved a higher level of obedience to God than the apostle Paul enjoyed when he was writing the Epistle to the Romans?"

To my everlasting shock the young man replied without flinching, "Yes!" Such is the extent to which persons will delude themselves into thinking that they have achieved sinlessness.

I spoke once with a woman who claimed the same "second blessing" of perfectionism who qualified her claim a bit. She said that she was fully sanctified into holiness so that she never committed any willful sins. But she acknowledged that occasionally she still committed sins, though never willfully. Her present sins were unwillful.

What in the world is an unwillful sin? All sin involves the exercise of the will. If an action happens apart from the will it is not a moral action. The involuntary beating of my heart is not a moral action. All sin is willful. Indeed, the corrupt inclination of the will is of the very essence of sin. There is no sin without the willing of sin. The woman was excusing her own sin by denying that she had willed to commit the sin. The sin just sort of "happened." It was the oldest self-justification known to man: "I didn't mean to do it!"

In one strand of the Wesleyan tradition there is another type of qualified perfectionism. Here the achievement of perfection is limited to a perfected *love*. We may continue to struggle with certain moral weaknesses, but at least we can receive the blessing of a perfected love. But think on this a moment. If we received the blessing of a love that was absolutely perfect, how then would we ever commit any kind of sin? If I ever loved God perfectly, I would will only obedience to Him. How could a creature who loved God perfectly ever sin against Him at all?

Someone might answer: "We could still sin against Him in ignorance." But the perfect love with which we are called to love God is a perfect love of our minds as well as our hearts. If we perfectly loved God with all of our minds, from whence could this ignorance flow? One who loves God *perfectly* with the mind is perfectly diligent in studying and mastering the Word of God. The perfectly loving mind perceives correctly the light into our paths. A perfectly loving mind doesn't make errors in understanding Scripture.

But could we not still make mistakes because our minds are less than perfect? I ask why our minds are less than perfect. It is not because we lack brains or the faculty of thinking. Our thinking is clouded because our hearts are clouded. Take away the cloud from our hearts and our minds are illumined by the clear light of God.

A perfect love would yield perfect obedience. The only perfected love this world has ever seen was the love of Christ, who exhibited perfect obedience. Jesus loved the Father perfectly. He sinned not at all, either willfully or in ignorance.

THE BIBLICAL VIEW

In Romans 7:14, Paul declares: "I am carnal, sold under sin." Does this mean that Paul was a carnal Christian? Did Paul receive Christ as Savior and not as Lord? To ask such foolish questions is to answer them. The world has never seen a more Spirit-filled Christian than the apostle Paul. Yet he said, "I am carnal."

When Paul declares that he is carnal, he is expressing the ongoing struggle in the Christian life between the old man and the new man, the warfare that goes on between the flesh and the Spirit. He summarizes his struggle with these words:

For I delight in the law of God according to the inward man. But I see another law in my members, warring against the law of my mind, and bringing me into captivity to the law of sin which is in my members. O wretched man that I am! Who will deliver me from this body of death? I thank God—through Jesus Christ our Lord! So then, with the mind I myself serve the law of God, but with the flesh the law of sin. Romans 7:22-25

We notice that Paul ends this expression of personal struggle with doxology. He utters praise and thanksgiving to God through Christ for the deliverance that we have in the inward man.

In the popular booklet published by Campus Crusade for Christ called "The Holy Spirit Booklet" (or, affectionately, the "Bird Book" because of the image of the dove that adorns its cover), mention is made of distinction between the carnal Christian and the Spirit-filled Christian. On the surface it appears as if Dr. Bill Bright is teaching an absolute distinction between two kinds of Christians. I am confident, however, that is not the intention of the booklet or of its author. Rather, in a pastoral way, Dr. Bright is discussing the classical struggle here between the flesh and the Spirit that every genuine Christian faces. The point of the booklet is to call us to exercise the power of the Holy Spirit in our lives in order to keep the evil tendencies of the old man in check. The old man is to be put to death daily. Victory comes in the Christian life by keeping our eyes upon the Spirit who is to reign over our possessions. Here the struggle is transcended as we look to Christ, the Author and Finisher of our faith.

All Christians are "carnal" insofar as we continue to struggle with the old nature of flesh. But no true Christian is carnal in the sense that the flesh totally dominates his life. If the carnal aspect were in total dominion, we would know that we were still unregenerate. We are called to live a Spirit-filled life in order to be victorious over the old man. It is precisely because of the residual power of sin that we need the filling of the Holy Spirit. We please God by asking for this holy filling. He is pleased with us—not when we express our joy at our "perfect" state—but when we express our need of Him and our dissatisfaction with the "body of death" that, thanks be to Him, is steadily growing less important in the Christian's life.

CHAPTER ELEVEN
THE SIN OF PRIDE

Karl Barth once declared that fallen man has three primary or basic sins from which all other sins proceed. These three sins include pride *(hubris)*, slothfulness, and dishonesty. Whether Barth is correct in his evaluation is arguable, but there is no doubt that this triad of vices is indeed formidable. They raise their ugly heads in a multitude of ways, bringing to ruin our efforts to achieve true godliness.

In this chapter we will consider the first of the three, pride. Perhaps the classic biblical quotation on pride is this oft-quoted section from Proverbs: "Pride goes before destruction, and a haughty spirit before a fall. Better to be of a humble spirit with the lowly, than to divide the spoil with the proud" (Proverbs 16:18-19).

Pride goes before destruction. Destruction is a description of collapse. People can be moving forward, building empires or reputations, riding high. It all collapses when pride undermines a sound foundation. The plaintive cry of the fallen is "I am ruined." It is a dreadful cry, a mournful whimper of those who make a wreck of their lives.

One morning I had a humorous experience with pride. At the break of dawn my wife and I went to the supermarket. As we pulled into the parking lot, Vesta said to me, "I hope you don't expect me to get out of the car. I have some pride, you know." Vesta was reluctant to leave the car because of her predawn appearance. She was wearing sweatpants, a man's large sweatshirt, and no makeup. She had not yet combed her hair. "I have some pride, you know," she said. I looked at her and with a mischievous grin said, "I have one question." "What's that?" she asked. Looking at her attire, I said, "Why?"

She was ready to hit me over the head with a book. She proved Luther's famous quote he once made concerning his beloved wife, Katy Von Bora: "If God wanted me to have a meek woman, He'd have to hew one out of stone!"

But the kind of pride Vesta was declaring was not the pride of which the Bible speaks. There is nothing evil in "taking pride in your work" or in wanting to "look your best." These matters are simple concerns of human dignity. There is no sin in wanting to do a quality job. The striving after excellence is a virtue, not a vice. To feel good about one's work is to achieve the sense of satisfaction of a job well done. God Himself looked at the work of His own hands and said, "That's good." Here the deity was not puffed up in arrogance on the way to His own divine destruction.

Proverbs links pride with a haughty spirit, a spirit of insufferable arrogance. The arrogant have a cocky stance about them. We all recognize it when we see it. We remember the warning from Scripture about those things that are repugnant to God: "These six things the LORD hates, Yes, seven are an abomination to Him: A proud look . . ." (Proverbs 6:16-17a).

The destructive pride born of arrogance is evident in the most destructive episode in human history. This event is not referred to simply as "a" fall but is described as "the" Fall, the fall of the entire human race.

In the Garden of Eden the first sin was a sin of pride. The temptation of the serpent came with these words: "You will be like God" (Genesis 3:5). It is one thing to strive for excellence. It is another to seek equal status with God.

The lust for power and dominance among men knows no limits. We are vulnerable to the temptation to achieve status above all men. We want to be able to declare our opinions without the need to defend them. "Because I say so" is an argument that ultimately is valid only for God.

The temptation to be like God is greater than we think. We resist being subject to law. We squirm when we are placed under too much authority. We love to be free—free of restraints, free of accountability.

THE QUEST FOR AUTONOMY

Freedom is indeed a precious commodity. But our freedom has limits. The fact is we are under restraints and we are accountable. We are ultimately answerable to God. We are simply not permitted to do everything we want to do.

Recently I was riding in a car with a friend. We found ourselves traveling the wrong direction on a city street. A sign at the intersection read, "No U-Turn." My friend promptly made a U-turn and proceeded in the other direction. When I voiced a protest at this lawless action he said to me, "R. C., you can't be intimidated by a metal sign."

This was the expression of a "scofflaw." I thought at once of the biblical mandate to obey the civil magistrates. Certainly there are times when civil laws seem to reflect bureaucratic incompetence more than justice, but we are still called to avoid the complex of lawlessness. My obedience to law is not rendered to a metal sign. It is to be offered to Christ as an indication of my willingness to be in subjection to the authorities He establishes.

Obviously there are times when Christians not only may but must disobey the civil authorities, but such civil disobedience requires a just and necessary reason. We may not disobey the law willy-nilly simply because the law inconveniences us. To do so is to set ourselves above the law, which is a symptom of destructive pride.

Our quest to be like God is a quest to be above law. It is the quest for autonomy. Autonomy means literally "self-law." A person who seeks to be utterly autonomous is a person who seeks to be a law unto himself. He is answerable to no one.

We must be careful here. To avoid autonomy does not mean that we seek to be under tyranny. There are authority structures set down in Scripture that define appropriate lines of accountability. Children are to submit to their parents, employees to employers, the sheep to their shepherd, students to their teachers, and so on. We all are unavoidably cast into some type of human relationships in which we must either exercise authority or submit to it.

We must be wary of tyrants in disguise who seek to place us under authority where God has left us free. It is not arrogant for parents to refuse to submit to the authority of their children or for teachers to refuse to submit to their students. That is not being "accountable"; it is being manipulated.

I am fearful of people who are forever talking about being "accountable." The concept can be an insidious device of manipulation, a favorite tool of control managers who want to extend their own authority beyond valid limits.

I once talked to a man who owned his own business. He remarked, "I hold my board meetings in the shower." What he meant was this: As president and owner of his company he was at the apex of authority in the organization. He was the boss. The buck stopped with him. This did not mean that he was a man without accountability. He was accountable to his bank. He was accountable to the law of his community and state. He was accountable to his elders and pastor in his church. He was accountable ultimately to God. But he was not under the authority of his secretary. She was under his authority, at the office.

It is important for the Christian to know precisely what authority he is under and then to be subject to that authority with a willing spirit. Part of my vows of ordination to the ministry require that I take a solemn oath before God to be in subjection to the authority of my church. We acknowledge that the church cannot bind my conscience. Only God can bind my conscience. If I have a conscientious objection to the rule of my church in which I face the dilemma of obeying the church or obeying God, then I must obey God. If my disobedience to the church is of such magnitude as to disturb the peace and unity of the church, then it is my duty to withdraw from that body in peace.

The same applies to working relationships. I am to be in

subjection to my authorities unless I am constrained by conscience to disobey. If such disobedience is intolerable to my employer, then I must seek work elsewhere.

When we find ourselves in such tension, we must be careful to search our hearts and make sure our objection is really motivated by a godly conscience. It is easy to camouflage a prideful resistance with a spiritual cloak of hypocrisy.

THE QUEST FOR STATUS

There is no occasion more painful to our pride than when we are treated beneath our dignity. We work to achieve certain levels of human respect. We want to be treated with a level of dignity commensurate with our status. Status seeking seems to be an integral dimension of American life. But it is by no means limited to America. It is a human phenomenon. The chief of a primitive tribe of natives is as jealous to guard the extra feathers in his bonnet as the manager is to guard his key to the executive washroom.

When I enrolled in the Free University of Amsterdam, I was given an instruction booklet on the proper protocol for formal titles of my professors. If the professor was from an upper-class family, he was to be addressed as "very well-born." If he had a graduate degree, he was "very well-learned." If he was ordained, he was "highly worthy." The string of titles was at best cumbersome. Two lines of print were necessary to address an envelope to some of these titled men. Woe to the student who failed to use the proper title.

I thought this system of titles was one of the silliest things I had ever encountered. It came down to status of cars on the highway. Volkswagens were expected to yield the right of way to Mercedes. I once witnessed a truck pull up beside a bicyclist at a stoplight. The truck slowly nudged over toward the bicycle until the driver intentionally nudged the bike over to the ground because the cyclist would not yield the right of way to the truck.

This obsession with status is, alas, contagious. After I lived in this culture for a time I received a letter in the mail addressed to De Heer Sproul. I was miffed. "De Heer!" I was worthy of far more titles than that! I felt like I was being addressed as "occupant." Then it suddenly dawned on me that I was getting caught up in the status game.

I would like to report that my flirtation with status seeking ended in Amsterdam. But it didn't. Just recently I was in a shopping mall with my son. We stopped to browse in a jewelry store. I found myself looking enviously at a display of Rolex watches. I said to my son, "I sure would like to have a Rolex watch."

My son registered shock. "Gee, Dad," he said, "I can understand wanting to spend money on things that could bring some comfort to your life, but why would you want to buy something just for status?"

I was stung by his words. I was ready to launch into a speech about aesthetics. I wanted to say, "It's just a matter of beauty. I like beautiful things." The speech would have been a half-truth. I do like beautiful things. I love art. But I knew in my heart of hearts that the Rolex did not fit that category for me. My son was right. I was taken with the name "Rolex" and what it represents. It was a matter of status, and I was not too "proud" of myself for the realization.

The great hymn of *kenosis* (self-emptying) in Philippians 2 speaks to this issue. Hear the words of the apostle Paul:

Let nothing be done through selfish ambition or conceit, but in lowliness of mind let each esteem others better than himself. Let each of you look out not only for his own interests, but also for the interests of others.
Philippians 2:3-4

This introduction to the hymn is a hard saying. We are preoccupied with the issue of self-esteem. Yet here we are called to esteem others better than ourselves. This is precisely the opposite of our normal patterns. We usually want to think of ourselves as better than others. We want other people to esteem us as better than themselves.

This is part of the primordial temptation to be as gods. In the film *Hoosiers*, actor Gene Hackman, playing the role of a new coach in a small Indiana town, responds to the charge that too much importance is being given to basketball in the school. His antagonist complains that basketball players are being treated as gods. Hackman replies, "Don't you understand that men would kill to be treated like God for just a few minutes?"

That is self-esteem run amok. It is self-esteem tottering on the brink of destruction. It is the opposite of the lowliness of mind to which we are called.

TRUE HUMILITY

Such a high calling to humility might easily be dismissed as an idealistic abstract ethic with no real example in concrete life. But Paul doesn't leave it in an abstract realm. He moves quickly to the hymn that celebrates the supreme example of lowliness of mind as it was displayed in the life of Christ:

Let this mind be in you which was also in Christ Jesus, who, being in the form of God, did not consider it robbery to be equal with God, but made Himself of no reputation, taking the form of a servant, and coming in the likeness of men. And being found in appearance as a man, He humbled Himself and became obedient to the point of death, even the death of the cross. Therefore God also has highly exalted Him and given Him the name which is above every name. Philippians 2:5-9

We are called to share the mind of Christ. He emptied Himself in the Incarnation. He did not empty Himself of His deity or any of His divine attributes. He emptied Himself of His *status*. He set aside His prerogatives as God. He was willing to be treated beneath the level of His dignity. This example of the man with the highest dignity ever possessed by a human shames every other human who sets pride above obedience.

We remember King Saul. Saul was selected by God to be the first king of Israel. The king of Israel was not to be given autonomous authority. He was subject to the divine King's law. No earthly monarch could supplant the ultimate ruler of the nation, Yahweh. Yahweh was the Jews' God and King.

Saul got off to a good beginning, but soon he grew puffed up with his own importance. He took to himself the prerogatives of the priest and supplanted the role of Samuel (1 Samuel 13:9). He grew more selfish and arrogant. His jealousy reached a peak when the people began to praise the exploits of the young David with the song: "Saul has slain his thousands, and David his ten thousands" (1 Samuel 18:7). What follows is a history of Saul's pathetic dementia.

Saul's life ended in tragedy. After being severely wounded in battle with the Philistines, Saul took his own life by falling upon his sword. His enemies cut off his head and hung his body on a wall as a public spectacle.

David lamented the death of Saul and instructed the children of Judah to learn the Song of the Bow: "The beauty of Israel is slain on your high places! How the mighty have fallen! Tell it not in Gath. Proclaim it not in the streets of Ashkelon" (2 Samuel 1:19-20).

Throughout the song the mournful refrain is repeated: "How the mighty have fallen."

The life of Saul is a clear example of the Proverb: Pride goes before destruction and a haughty spirit before a fall. Mighty power begets mighty pride. Mighty pride begets a mighty fall.

The lure of status is powerful. It looms as a dreadful obstacle to Christian growth. We are all so vulnerable to it. No one wants to live like Rodney Dangerfield. We all crave the respect of others. Sigmund Freud once told the story of a schoolboy who was expelled from school for misbehavior. He stood outside the classroom and threw pebbles against the windows. Finally the principal went outside and confronted the boy: "Why are you throwing pebbles against the windows?" he asked. The boy replied, "I just wanted everyone to know that I'm still here."

We all carry pebbles in our pockets. We want to save "face." We want to keep our self-esteem intact. We fear humiliation. Our pride is a powerful force.

During the Cuban missile crisis of the early 1960s, President Kennedy demanded the removal of Russian military rockets from Cuba. The United States dispatched vessels to Cuba. At the same time Nikita Khrushchev ordered the Soviet fleet toward Cuba.

The world held its breath. Walter Cronkite gave hourly bulletins on the progress of the Soviet Fleet. The military powers seemed on a headlong course toward Armageddon. At the last moment Russia blinked. The Soviet ships veered off and returned home. It was a great triumph for Kennedy. It was a total disgrace for Khrushchev, ultimately leading to his fall from power.

Then what happened? Kennedy had demanded on-site inspections in Cuba. Khrushchev refused, and Kennedy withdrew his demand. When the press asked President Kennedy why he had backed down on the demand he said, "We have won the dispute. It was important to give

R · C · S P R O U L

the Soviet premier a graceful exit."

Kennedy's diplomacy was directed toward preserving some of Khrushchev's pride. He did not want to back the premier into a corner where he had no dignity left. I shudder to think what could have happened had Kennedy been less sensitive. The pride issue in that confrontation might have led to the very destruction of the world.

What place does pride have in the Christian life? None. In a fallen world, premiers and presidents must play their games of face-saving and exhibition of status. We know that this is the way the world works. But we hark back to the hymn in Philippians 2, where Paul exalts the humility of Christ while telling the Philippian Christians to imitate their Lord. Obedience, humility, the steady withering of pride and arrogance—these things appear foolish in a world that values status and esteem. But we have it on good authority that pleasing the Ruler of the universe means holding to values different from the world's. He certainly gave us the supreme example of what it means to live humbly. He did not just teach us to shun pride—He showed us how.

CHAPTER TWELVE

THE SIN

OF

SLOTHFULNESS

God is a God of work. The Bible's first description of God gives us a glimpse of God in the act of creation. He is the original and supreme producer. He is the fountainhead of all productivity.

Because the curse of the fall of man stresses unpleasant aspects of work, many have jumped to the conclusion that work itself is part of man's curse. But we see that before sin entered the world man and woman were given a task to perform by their Creator.

As soon as God created man, He planted a garden eastward in Eden. God made the trees grow there in abundance. Then God gave man the responsibility to take care of the garden: "Then the LORD God took the man and put him in the garden of Eden to tend and keep it" (Genesis 2:15).

At this point there were no thorns, briars, and weeds in the garden. Imagine taking care of a garden where there were no weeds. Adam's gardening chores were the fun type—pruning, picking the fruit, trimming, and the like. He didn't have to fight the never-ending battle with weeds. There were no thorns to get stuck between his fingernail and his skin. He could take care of the daily chores, have the assurance of a full yield of fruit, and never work up a drop of sweat. Before the Fall, God was pleased to have man working in the garden. It was a pleasant work, pleasant for man to do, and pleasant for the Creator to watch.

Once sin came into the world, everything changed. Caring for a garden became a matter of difficult labor. Here is the curse of Adam:

Cursed is the ground for your sake; in toil you shall eat of it all the days of your life. Both thorns and thistles it shall bring forth for you, and you shall eat the herb of the field. In the sweat of your face you shall eat bread till you return to the ground, for out of it you were taken; for dust you are, and to dust you shall return. Genesis 3:17-19

Here are the elements of the curse: thorns, thistles, sweat, and death. Here is the origin of the triad of human pain: blood, sweat, and tears. Yet, as we shall see, the curse is not work itself. After the Fall, as before, work is a divine mandate. God is pleased to see His human creature working.

MAN THE WORKER
When we consider our humanity we usually define ourselves as *homo sapiens*, "man the wise" or "man the thinking animal." We point to our thought patterns as our most distinctive characteristic.

Karl Marx wasn't satisfied with that definition. He preferred another Latin name—*homo faber*. This is "man the maker" or "man the worker." Marx was convinced that labor is so integral to human life that the very definition of man is tied to his labor. In other words, work is not a curse. It is something that to an enormous degree defines who we are and brings (or *should* bring) satisfaction and meaning.

At that point Marx was not completely wrong. When we meet people for the first time we usually go through a three-step routine. We ask each other three questions: "What is your name?" "Where do you live?" and "What do you do?" Name, address, occupation—these are the three factors that define a person in our culture.

What we do is bound up with our total self-identity. How we do what we do is equally important. We are constantly being judged on our performance at our jobs. In one sense we are all like the major-league baseball player whose batting average changes with each fresh turn at the bat. If the player's average slips below a certain point, his job is in jeopardy. His livelihood is tied to his job. All of us face the trials of the relationship of life and labor. We must work to live, and, more than just working, we must perform reasonably well.

Yet work is to have a higher purpose than self-preservation. With Adam we are all called by God to be productive. We are called to bear fruit. To be productive and fruitbearing people we must be willing to work with dedication.

A refusal to work is a refusal to participate in one of the most fundamental human duties. We groan at times under the burden of the curse, but the thorns, briars, and sweat do not excuse us from our vocation.

The very word *vocation* comes from the Latin *vocare*, "to call." Our vocation is a calling; it is a calling from God.

To shirk our vocation is to run from our duty. We must work.

SLOTH AND POVERTY

Sloth is the enemy of productivity. The slothful person not only injures himself but is a burden to society. Not only does the slothful person fail to add to the productivity of his society, but he begins to live off other people's labor. This is the antisocial dimension of sloth—the lazy person expects to be cared for by the diligent.

The society's responsibility toward the handicapped does not carry over to the able-bodied. The Bible has much to say about the poor and the church's responsibility toward the poor. We err grievously, however, if we fail to distinguish among the various types of poor people mentioned in Scripture. Scripture distinguishes among at least *four* types of poverty.

Poverty as a Result of Calamity: There are those who are poor because they have been the victims of some catastrophe. They have been rendered incapable of productivity by disease, injury, flood, or some other natural disaster. To these people the Christian is called to open his heart in loving assistance. We are responsible to bring relief to these stricken people.

Poverty as a Result of Oppression: Some people experience poverty as a result of being victims of unjust people of power. They may be victimized by theft, extortion, or brutality. Perhaps they have been sold into slavery and have been treated as animals. Perhaps they are orphans and widows who are being exploited.

These people's oppressors cause God to thunder in anger. He will not tolerate the oppression and exploitation of the weak. The history of Israel as a nation began when God heard the groans of an enslaved people and demanded of the pharaoh of Egypt, "Let my people go!"

Poverty for the Kingdom's Sake: There are those who are poor because they choose to be poor. They voluntarily divest themselves of worldly goods. They are the Mother Teresas of this world who resolve to live at a bare subsistence level in order to provide more relief to the needy. Although this life-style is by no means required by God, it nevertheless evokes a certain delight in God. This kind of poverty is noble. Its virtuous motivation is indeed noteworthy.

Therefore, we see three distinct groups of poor people who are by no means under the judgment of God. It is the fourth group that provokes God's wrath. It is the fourth group whose poverty is an expression and consequence of their sin.

Poverty Because of Sloth: This fourth category of the poor does not awaken the compassion of God. On the contrary, God's wrath is kindled against the indolent. Note the words of Proverbs:

Go to the ant, you sluggard! Consider her ways and be wise, which, having no captain, overseer or ruler, provides her supplies in the summer, and gathers her food in the harvest. How long will you slumber, O sluggard? When will you rise from your sleep? A little sleep, a little slumber, a little folding of the hands to sleep—So shall your poverty come on you like a robber, and your need like an armed man. Proverbs 6:6-11

"Just a little nap, forty winks. I'll do it tomorrow." Play now, work later is the creed of the sluggard. The ant, by contrast, prepares for the winter in the summer. Her storehouses are full when the bitter weather comes.

Again the Proverbs speak:

He who deals with a slack hand becomes poor, but the hand of the diligent makes one rich. He who gathers in summer is a wise son, but he who sleeps in harvest is a son who causes shame. Proverbs 10:4-5

The wisdom literature of the Old Testament abounds with references to slothfulness. Let us note merely a few passages in passing: "He who is slothful in his work is a brother to him who is a great destroyer" (Proverbs 18:9). "A slothful man buries his hand in the bowl, and will not so much as bring it to his mouth again" (Proverbs 19:24). "The desire of the slothful kills him, for his hands refuse to labor" (Proverbs 21:25). "The slothful man says, 'There is a lion outside! I shall be slain in the streets!'" (Proverbs 22:13). "Because of laziness the building decays, and through idleness of hands the house leaks" (Ecclesiastes 10:18).

Such views are not limited to the Old Testament. The same negative judgment toward slothfulness is found in the New Testament. In the parable of the talents, the master speaks harshly to the unprofitable servant: "You wicked and lazy servant, you know that I reap where I have not sown, and gather where I have not scattered seed" (Matthew 25:26).

Perhaps the strongest indictment against the slothful anywhere in Scripture is found in Paul's Second Letter to the Thessalonians:

For even when we were with you, we commanded you this: If anyone will not work, neither shall he eat. For we hear that there are some who walk among you in a disorderly manner, not working at all, but are busybodies. 2 Thessalonians 3:10-11

No work, no food, is the apostle's mandate. Paul describes those who refuse to work as busybodies.

It is a strange term to use for malingerers. (Perhaps a more current word would be *loafers*.) Those who refused to work were still active. They were engaged in "hanging around" together joining in gossip. Their business was not a business of productivity.

THE WORKAHOLIC

The term *workaholic* is used in two quite different ways in our culture. In popular usage the word describes a hard-working person who hardly ever stops to rest and has little time in his busy schedule for recreation and social amenities.

But there is a second way in which the word is used. It is used in a technical sense by psychologists. Here the term *workaholic* describes a nonproductive busybody who accomplishes little or no real work. This type of workaholic looks very busy. He is busy at creating an illusion of work.

I remember a fellow in our college class who seemed to have a remarkable level of discipline in the matter of studying. It seemed that every hour we were out of class he was at his desk, hard at work studying. There were no idle visits to the student union building, no participation in dorm antics. There was no play.

Yet when exam time rolled around he always did very poorly. He sometimes flunked his tests. I was amazed that such a disciplined effort yielded such little fruit. Then one evening I was able to observe my friend while he was "studying." He sat at his desk, his head propped up by his hands, intently staring at the book in front of him. His eyes were glazed. I watched for several minutes as he gazed blankly at the page. He didn't turn a page. He was at the desk. His eyes were on the book, but his mind was obviously somewhere else. I thought I was observing a man sleeping with his eyes wide open.

The neurotic workaholic loves to give the appearance of hard work. Frequently he is the first to arrive at the office and the last to leave. His light stays on at night. He carries a heavy briefcase wherever he goes. Often he is a disruptive force in the office. He loves to criticize coworkers for their failures. He covers his own tracks efficiently by shifting blame to others. He always appears busy, but his most significant characteristic is that he never produces. He is busy doing either nothing or the trivial. His business is a substitute for productive labor.

We must be careful here. The nonproducing workaholic displays many characteristics of people who are diligent and productive. Simply because a person arrives early and works late does not identify him as a producer.

The counterfeit imitates the genuine except at the points of production and the assumption of responsibility. The bogus worker appears busy, but he is marked by the two fatal flaws of nonproduction and chronic buck-passing. His criticism of others is an attempt to mask his own failure. This type of workaholic is a slothful person in disguise. The workaholic often fools fellow workers—in fact, he may even fool himself. But he does not fool God, who surely takes no pleasure in seeing unproductive workers covering up their lack of productivity.

Many Christians have grown up with the idea that a person should always look busy. Sociologists and historians have debated for years about the source of the so-called Protestant work ethic, but there is a general agreement that Protestants in northern Europe and America have often had an exalted view of work. Far from seeing it as a curse, many of us have been taught to see it as the great goal of life. The problem is that, where such a view prevails, there are still people who are lazy and unproductive. They don't want to be perceived that way, so they cover their tracks. These people burden themselves (and others) not only with their unproductive habits but also with constant patterns of deception.

THE SWEET SLEEP OF THE WORKER

That we must work is a divine command. *That* we work and not be slothful is a moral matter. *Where* we work is a matter of prudence. The virtuous person is a working person. The wise person is one who marries his motivated ability pattern to his job.

Obviously it is not always possible to find a perfect job fit for our abilities. But much guilt and frustration can be avoided if we seek to know ourselves and seek as much as it is possible to find a good match in our jobs. Even in situations where we do not feel matched to our jobs, however, we are still under a divine mandate to work well. God is pleased to see us in jobs that are perfectly matched to our talents and needs, but He is also pleased that we work with dedication in whatever situation we find ourselves.

The Bible says that the sleep of a working man is sweet (Ecclesiastes 5:12). Productive work may be tiresome, but it is also highly satisfying. It makes for a sleep that is not disturbed by fits of anxiety and frustration.

Anxious sleep often results from the guilt we feel for shirking our responsibilities. The anxiety builds up in direct proportion to the work we leave undone. I knew a women who suffered from severe bouts of depression. She was under the care of a psychiatrist. Her depression attacks were finally seen to have a direct correlation to the amount of unironed clothes in her laundry basket. She hated to iron, and her family did not wear wash-and-wear clothes. As the clothes piled up in the laundry basket, so did her anxiety until she reached a fever pitch of depression.

I can relate to that. Though I'm not yet under the care of a psychiatrist, I feel anxiety related to unanswered mail. I hate to answer my mail. The more my mail stacks up, the worse I feel. It is a point of sloth in my life that brings the consequence of depressing guilt.

I once had an economics professor who, once a semester, stood on top of his desk and shouted his favorite law of economics: "You gotta work!" He got our attention. His manner of preaching may have been unorthodox, but with one sentence he captured the spirit of the Law of God. Work is our duty. It is our divine vocation. Each of us has a task to perform.

I can think of no words sweeter to the ear than to hear the words of Jesus: "Well done, thou good and faithful servant." I long to hear those words someday. I am sure we all want to hear them. But if we are to receive that benediction from Christ, we must be diligent now, faithful to do the work He has called us to perform. In this we please Him.

CHAPTER THIRTEEN

THE SIN

OF

DISHONESTY

A ll men are liars," says Psalm 116:11. This is echoed in conclusion of the apostolic indictment of the human race. Paul declares: "Indeed, let God be true but every man a liar" (Romans 3:4).

Dishonesty is a severe problem with us. We violate the truth in our speech, our actions, and our relationships. We lie to each other, to God, and to ourselves. This problem is found early in human history. The first recorded lie is uttered by the serpent in Eden. When the Devil said to Eve, "You will not die," he was lying. It is the nature of Satan to lie. Jesus described Satan in this manner:

You are of your father the devil, and the desires of your father you want to do. He was a murderer from the beginning, and does not stand in the truth, because there is no truth in him. When he speaks a lie, he speaks from his own resources, for he is a liar and the father of it. John 8:44

The conflict between God and Satan is focused on the issue of truth. God is the fountainhead of all truth; Satan is the father of lies. The central issue between Christ and the Antichrist is the issue of truth. The prefix "anti" that describes the Antichrist can mean either "against" or "in place of." The Antichrist fights against Christ. His chief ploy is to seek to replace Christ. He asserts himself as a substitute for Christ. He is the counterfeit, the fraud who works to supplant the genuine article. The Antichrist is a

191

false Christ. In a word, he is a liar. He pretends to be something that he is not.

The Antichrist is the ultimate hypocrite. He is involved in the great deception. He performs lying signs and wonders. Everything about him is counterfeit. His goal is to undermine the truth, to obscure the truth from view. As Satan disguises himself as an angel of light, so the Antichrist tries to pass himself off as the Christ.

The Antichrist depends upon our cavalier attitude toward truth for his own power. He builds his kingdom upon the kind of lies that appeal to people who enjoy lies. We remember that in vivid contrast Jesus declared: "For this cause I was born, and for this cause I have come into the world, that I should bear witness to the truth. Everyone who is of the truth hears My voice" (John 18:37).

To be of the truth is to hear the voice of Christ. Christ is the very incarnation of truth. The battle between light and darkness, between Christ and Antichrist, is the battle between truth and falsehood.

As we made a brief survey of biblical passages concerning slothfulness, let us do the same with lying. The following represents a brief sampling of biblical comments:

These six things the LORD hates, yes, seven are an abomination to Him: A proud look, a lying tongue. . . (Proverbs 6:16-17). Lying lips are an abomination to the LORD, but those who deal truthfully are His delight (Proverbs 12:22). A righteous man hates lying, but a wicked man is loathsome and comes to shame (Proverbs 13:5). A poor man is better than a liar (Proverbs 19:22).

*All liars shall have their part in the lake which burns
with fire and brimstone, which is the second death
(Revelation 21:8).*

LYING TO OTHERS

When we lie we usually do it to other people. We are
motivated to lie by several factors. We note that lying is
closely related to the other sins of pride and slothfulness.
We lie to others because we fear that truth will injure our
esteem. When our pride cannot bear that the truth be
known about us, we cover our tracks by lying. We lie to
escape punishment; we lie to cover up our guilt.

We also lie to hide our slothfulness. One of the most
widespread forms of lying is via cheating. We cheat to
conceal our lack of preparation. If we have not diligently
prepared for an examination, we resort to cheating as a
substitute for proper preparation. The grade we receive if
we are not caught is a dishonest grade. This is particularly
grievous when we cheat in competitive tests. Our cheating then becomes a form of stealing, as others are penalized
by our dishonesty.

The golfer who cheats in a tournament steals from the
other players who are the victims of the dishonesty. Thus
by cheating we do violence to the truth and violate other
people.

I am ashamed to recount an incident in which I was
involved in college. I had a friend who had great difficulty
with the study of Greek. Before every test we met togeth-

er and I tutored him rigorously to help him get ready. He was barely passing as we came down to the wire, the final exam. During the final exam the professor left the room, leaving us on our "honor." We did not act in an honorable way.

My friend was seated next to me. As he got farther into the exam his anxiety increased. He began to crane his neck to look at my paper. I helped him. I pushed my paper to the side of my desk so that he could get a clear view of it. I was obviously a willing accomplice in the deed.

When the exam grades were posted on the professor's office door, two grades were conspicuously absent. There was an asterisk next to my name and my friend's, with a note to "see the professor." My heart was pounding as I knocked on the professor's door.

The professor ushered me into his office. To my sick astonishment he produced a chart of every answer of every student to every question. The chart revealed that on several questions two people and only two people had the same wrong answer. The evidence was incontrovertible. The professor looked at me sadly and said, "I have just one question for you." "Yes, sir?" I replied. "Are the answers on your paper your own?" I replied, "Yes, but—" I started to confess my complicity in the scandal. He cut me off in mid-sentence.

"I don't want to hear it," the professor said. "All I want to know is, are your answers your own?" Again I said "Yes," and he promptly dismissed me.

For reasons I do not understand but for which I am still

grateful, the professor gave me no penalties. I received his utter mercy. My friend did not fare so well. He received an F for the entire course. The results were an academic disaster for him.

We both cheated. My help was motivated simply by compassion for his panic. I know that I took pride in his achievement because I was coaching him. I was cheating as much for me as I was for him. Either way we were being dishonest. I resolved from that day never to cheat on an exam in any way.

I also became sensitive to the temptations of cheating. I was later in charge of a youth group in a church. I had about thirty young people in the class. On one occasion I said to them, "OK, let's get real honest here. How many of you ever cheat on tests?"

I was shocked by the response. Every hand in the room went up. I don't know if I was more shocked by the fact that they all did it or by the fact that they were all willing to admit it.

We then proceed to a lengthy discussion about *why* they cheated. The answers they gave included: "My parents put so much pressure on me to make good grades, . . ." "Every one else is cheating and it is the only way I can compete." "I don't want to look stupid." "The tests aren't fair."

We talked it out. As a group we resolved to change our habits. For the entire semester I asked them each week: "Did you cheat this week?" Some of them stopped cheating immediately. Others struggled with it deeply. What emerged was a camaraderie among them whereby they were encouraging each other toward honesty.

Not all lies to others are connected with our pride and slothfulness. Some are related to our desire for unjust gain. Salesmen, for example, seem to forget that under normal circumstances they are expected to tell the truth. For example, on a business transaction the truth is due to the buyer. They cannot hide behind a convenient policy of *caveat emptor* ("Let the buyer beware"). If my car has a hidden mechanical problem, it is my duty to make full disclosure of that when I go to sell it. It is fraud to sell things by false representation. The truth is due the buyer.

Only recently has the law in the United States required truth in lending and truth in advertising. Lenders can no longer conceal hidden costs with impunity. Advertisers are now libel if they make false claims about their products. To lie in lending, advertising, or selling is to be involved in a not so subtle form of theft.

LYING ABOUT OTHERS

It is one thing to lie *to* others. It is still another matter to lie *about* others. This involves slander. To tell lies about other people is to cause them grave injury. The Devil himself is the master of slander. He encourages his disciples to engage in gossip, backbiting, and slander. To steal a person's good name may be more harmful to the person than to steal their property.

God is so concerned about slander and lying about others that He included a prohibition against it in His Ten

Commandments: "You shall not bear false witness against your neighbor" (Exodus 20:16).

The prohibition includes more than falsely accusing someone in a law court. The responsibility in Israel to tell the truth, the whole truth and nothing but the truth in a law court was taken very seriously. If perjury was committed in the courts, the penalties ranged all the way to the death penalty.

Justice cannot be maintained in the land unless the courts can be certain of the honesty of witnesses. But on a more daily basis, injurious lies can take the form of slander. Let us consider briefly the meaning and force of the verb "to slander." To slander someone is to tell lies about him, lies that injure him. Slander involves making an unjust accusation. We have all felt the sting of being slandered. It is one thing to suffer injury for sins of which we are guilty. It is another thing to be punished for something we did not do. No one enjoys the pain of false accusation.

Jesus was a victim of slander throughout His entire public ministry. Even in the agony of death He was subjected to verbal abuse. During His crucifixion He was the subject of debate between the two thieves that were executed with Him. "Then one of the criminals who were hanged blasphemed Him, saying, 'If You are the Christ, save Yourself and us' " (Luke 23:39).

Indeed Jesus was the Christ. There was no "if" about it. Here the accusation against Him, which was made in mockery, was ironically true. The mocking of the first thief was an attempt to slander Jesus. The response of the second thief was noteworthy:

197

But the other, answering, rebuked him, saying, "Do you not even fear God, seeing you are under the same condemnation? And we indeed justly, for we receive the due reward of our deeds; but this Man has done nothing wrong." Luke 23:40-41

Here the second thief acknowledged that his own punishment was just. He was guilty of the crimes for which he was being crucified. The other thief was likewise guilty. They were receiving justice. They were receiving what was *due* them. But Jesus was innocent of the charges against Him. He was a victim of false accusation. The cross—the central moment of all redemptive history—was, from a divine vantage point, the critical moment of salvation. Yet, from a human standpoint, it was the most vicious act of injustice ever committed in this world. It was the supreme act of slander in human history. Roman justice had declared that the innocent Son of God was worthy of death. The Jews, God's chosen people, those who expected a Messiah, had handed an innocent man over to the Romans.

The second thief set the record straight. "This man has done nothing amiss." Here the thief echoed the judgment of the Roman procurator, Pontius Pilate: "I have found no fault in this Man" (Luke 23:14). But Pilate, despite vindicating Jesus with these words, caved in to the clamoring crowd and allowed the punishment for the slanderous charges to be carried out. Pilate, acting as the Roman guardian of justice, spit in the face of justice to appease an angry mob.

However corrupt the second thief was, he used his last

breaths fighting for truth. He died with a testimony to justice and a plea for mercy on his lips: "Lord, remember me when You come into Your kingdom" (Luke 23:42).

Jesus was obviously touched that his integrity was being defended by such a man as this. He was quick to respond with a promise of grace: "Assuredly, I say to you, today you will be with me in Paradise" (Luke 23:43).

I suspect that the thief is still with Jesus in paradise. The Devil is not. There is no room for slander in the kingdom of Christ.

I labor the point of slander's being an injurious lie because it is one of the chief works of the Devil against God's people. To slander a person is to injure that person's reputation. Our reputations, our "good names," are important to our lives. Life is difficult enough without trying to operate with an evil reputation.

LIES FOR A GOOD PURPOSE

Jacob was a supplanter. He lived up to his name by stealing his brother Esau's birthright. The theft took place by deception. When Isaac grew old and was blind Jacob disguised himself by putting animal skins on his body and, posing as his hairy brother Esau, fooled Isaac into giving him the patriarchal blessing. All of this was done with the help and guidance of Isaac's wife Rebekah. She was the Mother of the lie:

Now therefore, my son, obey my voice according to what I command you. Go now to the flock and bring me from there two choice kids of the goats, and I will make savory food from them for your father, such as he loves. Then you shall take it to your father, that he may eat it, and that he may bless you before his death. Genesis 27:8-10

It might be argued that Rebekah was merely carrying out the will of God. God had ordained that the elder would serve the younger. Jacob was the child of promise. Rebekah was simply making sure that God's sovereign will was done.

However, God does not require the sins of humans to accomplish His holy will. He stands sovereign over sin but is not the author of sin. He accomplished His will through the example of Judas, but that did not absolve Judas of his crime. As in the case of Joseph's brothers, they meant it for evil, but God meant it for good. So Rebekah is still responsible for her sin. Her sin provoked an endless bitterness, an ongoing hatred between Esau and Jacob that carried over to their descendants. We might even say that part of the bloody struggle in Palestine today has its roots in one woman's unscrupulous lie.

But what of the lie of Rahab the harlot? Rahab made it to the roll call of heroes in Hebrews 11:

By faith the harlot Rahab did not perish with those who did not believe, when she had received the spies with peace. Hebrews 11:31

We read of Rahab's trickery in Joshua 2:

Then the woman took the two men and hid them; and she said, "Yes, the men came to me, but I did not know where they were from. And it happened as the gate was being shut, when it was dark, that the men went out. Where the men went I do not know; pursue them quickly, for you may overtake them." Joshua 2:4-5

This is the record of a bold-faced lie. The issue is, then, was Rahab blessed by God because of her lie, or in spite of her lie? Some put Rahab in the same category as Rebekah, arguing that she was blessed in spite of the lie. This position assumes that lying is *always* wrong.

On the other hand we have the principle that we must tell the truth *when the truth is due.* This position assumes that the truth is not always due. That is, not everyone is entitled to the truth.

Let me illustrate. When I lived in Holland, I lived in a home of a woman who had endured five years of Nazi occupation during World War II. It was the policy of the Germans to arrest young Dutchmen and ship them off to camps or to work projects for the Nazi war effort. This woman hollowed out a hiding place beneath the floorboards to hide her son. In this small cubicle she installed a ventilation fan and stored food provisions in the hiding place.

One day as the Nazis were searching the village for young men the woman hid her son beneath the floor. Without knocking, the soldiers burst into the house armed with submachine guns. They rushed to the bedroom and searched the closets for evidence of young men's clothing. They felt the beds to see if they were warm. Finally they returned to the living room and stood over the very spot where the son was hidden. A soldier said to the woman: "Are you hiding any boys here?"

What was her moral responsibility? Should she have said, "Yes there is one under the floor?" I think not. She had the moral right to lie. The Nazis had no right to the truth. She replied, "No, there are no boys here." Thereupon the soldiers began to shoot up the floor, all the while watching the Mother's reaction for any hint of panic. She displayed no outward emotion, while inside she was in stark terror.

Finally the soldiers left. Panic-stricken, the mother rushed to the hiding place. Her son emerged unscathed. Her deception had saved him.

We are not required to tell robbers where we have hidden our valuables. Soldiers are not required to tell the enemy where their comrades are positioned. Truth is to be told to those who are due it. We are not pleasing God when we tell the truth to people who do not deserve the truth.

LYING TO OURSELVES

One of the most difficult tasks we ever have is to tell the truth about ourselves to ourselves. On the surface it would seem incredible that this is difficult. Who knows more about ourselves than ourselves?

Yet the one person we must want to have a good opinion of ourself is ourself. It is painful in the extreme to face the darker side of our personalities with the stark truth. Usually it takes nothing less than the supernatural power of divine conviction for us to come to grips with personal reality. Indeed we are fortunate that the Holy Spirit does not reveal the full truth about ourselves to us all at once. Who could possibly bear such a full self-revelation? One glimpse of the holiness of God had Isaiah cursing himself. Job and Habakkuk almost perished when God gave them an unveiled view of themselves.

We lie to ourselves. We view our own actions in the best of all possible lights. Where we are quick to judge others harshly, we are equally quick to excuse ourselves. We are masters of the art of rationalization.

We remember David, a man after God's own heart. When he fell into sin with Bathsheba he called upon all of his cunning to mask his fault from himself. He added murder by proxy to his crime by using his authority to send Bathsheba's husband, Uriah, to the front lines in combat.

After taking Bathsheba for his own, David was confronted by the prophet Nathan. Nathan approached the king with a seemingly harmless parable:

Then the LORD sent Nathan to David. And he came to him, and said to him; "There were two men in one city, one rich and the other poor. The rich man had exceedingly many flocks and herds. But the poor man had nothing, except one little ewe lamb which he had bought and nourished; and it grew up together with him and with his children. It ate of his own food and drank from his own cup and lay in his bosom; and it was like a daughter to him.

And a traveler came to the rich man, who refused to take from his own flock and from his own herd to prepare one for the wayfaring man who had come to him; but he took the poor man's lamb and prepared it for the man who had come to him." 2 Samuel 12:1-4

When David heard this story from the prophet's lips he was furious. The narrative declares:

Then David's anger was greatly aroused against the man, and he said to Nathan, "As the LORD lives, the man who has done this shall surely die! And he shall restore fourfold for the lamb, because he did this thing and because he had no pity." 2 Samuel 12:5-6

Then Nathan, at the risk of his own life, put the sword deeply into David's soul. He cried out to the king: "You are the man!"

David was shattered. His repentance was as severe as his crime. He saturated his pillow with tears. Out of his stricken conscience he penned the immortal lines of the fifty-first Psalm. But David could not see his own guilt directly. Only when Nathan held up a mirror in front of him by disguising the sin could David see it. He recognized it clearly when it was cloaked in the story of another man's crime. Yet even then he did not make the personal application until Nathan pointed his finger in David's face.

David was not alone. In this tendency toward self-deceit, David is Everyman.

LYING TO GOD

We lie to others, we lie to ourselves. But our sin is compounded infinitely when we lie to God. Lying to God is as foolish as it is irreverent. It is foolish to think that we can deceive Him. Every secret thought in our heart is known to Him totally. No mountain is big enough to cover our guilt from His penetrating gaze.

We lie to God in a multitude of ways. Since Eden we have tried to conceal our shame by hiding from Him. We violate His truth. We break our covenants with Him. To swear an oath to God and to break it is to lie to Him.

The clearest example we have in Scripture of people lying to God is found in the story of Ananias and Sapphira:

But a certain man named Ananias, with Sapphira his wife, sold a possession. And he kept back part of the proceeds, his wife also being aware of it, and brought a certain part and laid it at the apostles' feet. But Peter said, "Ananias, why has Satan filled your heart to lie to the Holy Spirit and keep back part of the price of the land for yourself? While it remained, was it not your own? And after it was sold, was it not in your own control? Why have you conceived this thing in your heart? You have not lied to men but to God." Acts 5:1-4

As soon as the indictment was uttered by Peter, Ananias breathed his last. Moments later he was joined in death by his wife. The judgment of God was swift and decisive. He refused to tolerate this dishonesty.

Acts tells us that a result of the penalty imposed upon Ananias and Sapphira "great fear came upon all the church" (Acts 5:11).

The sin of Ananias and Sapphira was not that they refused to sell all of their possessions. That is not a universal requirement upon the church. Their sin was of lying. They made a pledge to God that they did not keep.

The healthy fear that gripped the church in the first century has long since evaporated. In the modern church we know that when pledges are made for giving, we cannot hope to receive more than eighty or eighty-five percent of the pledges made. The church still has the spirit of Ananias' lying to God.

Jesus came to bear witness to the truth. His people are called to be people of truth. As Christians we are to put away our fallen tendency to lie. We are to be done with lies. If we are to strive toward integrity, our striving must be toward truthfulness.

Truth is sacred because God is a God of truth. He has nothing to do with falsehood. His word can be trusted absolutely. We are to mirror that kind of fidelity to truth. We are to tell the truth, do the truth, and live the truth. In so doing we please the God of truth.

CHAPTER FOURTEEN
DOCTRINE
AND LIFE

Not doctrine, but *life*—that is what really matters. This is a sentiment often expressed in Christian circles. The idea is simple: God is less concerned about what we believe than He is about how we live. Creeds and dogma are unimportant. What matters is outward behavior. *Orthopraxy*, not *orthodoxy* is what counts. We may more completely please God with right behavior than with right thinking.

This is a false dilemma with perilous consequences. Right thinking and right living go together. We may distinguish them, but to separate them is deadly. We can have right theories without right practice. We can also have right practice without right theory, but only by accident as a happy inconsistency.

The disparaging of doctrine usually follows a common pattern. We begin by recognizing that there are people who have all the correct theological answers but who live scandalous lives. The Devil can make a high score on a theology test. It was the demons who first recognized Jesus as the Son of God before the disciples did, but the demons hated the truth they recognized so clearly. There are many people who know truth about God but who are living lives that could not possibly please God.

209

THE LEADERS' TREASON

There is a deep suspicion in the Christian community about theology, especially academic theology, and for good reason. The church has experienced what one scholar called "the treason of the intellectual." Much of the skepticism leveled against biblical Christianity has come from within the church. It was the church's theologians who declared the death of God. It is the theological seminaries that attack the trustworthiness of Scripture.

I remember my own rude awakening as a first-year seminary student. I was shocked to hear one of my professors not only deny the deity of Christ but attack it with a tone of hostility. I might have been less shocked had the professor expressed a deep personal crisis of faith in which he no longer could embrace the biblical faith. Had he made this confession with tears and a broken heart, I could have understood it. But his denial was couched in a kind of militancy against the biblical view of Jesus.

When I raised questions about this to him, my professor glared at me and said, "Young man, you have come to seminary with too many preconceived ideas." The preconceived idea for which I was rebuked was the belief in the deity of Christ.

I was bewildered. I naively assumed that everybody who went to a Christian seminary to prepare for the Christian ministry was already convinced of the deity of Christ. I couldn't imagine any other reason to be there. When I called attention to the fact that the creeds of our church clearly affirm the deity of Christ, the man replied (in private), "The orthodox creeds are full of ——." (He did not delete the expletive.)

Countless college students have had similar experiences with professors at church-related colleges. A natural reaction to the pain and shock of this kind of skepticism is to retreat into a nonintellectual haven of faith. The seductive temptation is to think, *If this is what academic theology produces, then who needs it? I'm going to keep my faith simple and avoid any involvement with theology.*

We must not assume that because someone is a theological scholar that he is a Christian. We may not assume that because someone is an ordained minister he is necessarily a Christian. Sadly, there are many people who enter the ministry for the wrong reasons. Some make theological skepticism a profession. There are those who are motivated to study Christian theology out of a burning desire to disprove, neutralize, or change Christianity. Natural man has enough enmity toward God to make a lifelong crusade against Him. There is an enemy within the church.

We have heard enough testimonies from clergy who declare they have been converted after their ordination to know that many are in fact ordained in unbelief. American colonial pastor Gilbert Tennent once wrote an essay entitled "The Dangers of an Unconverted Clergy." Tennent was not merely crying wolf. There are wolves out there in sheep's clothing. They masquerade as men and women of God while inwardly being at war with God. That is nothing new. We remember that the most hostile group toward Jesus in His earthly life was the clergy of his day, the scribes and the Pharisees.

People seek ordination for all sorts of reasons. One reason is to legitimatize their unbelief. Another reason, as we have seen, is to work against Christ from within. And there are many who are genuine humanitarians who see the church as a marvelous institution of social concern. Where else can a person find such a well-established platform for community influence?

When a businessman moves into a new community he must work hard at establishing new relationships. If he is to rise to a position of community prominence and influence, he must face the reality that it takes time and effort to do it. When a new minister comes to town he instantly steps into a position of community leadership. The influence of the local church may be waning, but it is still a reality. The minister has an instant platform from which to exert influence. He has a pulpit. He has a congregation. He has a church program. The wages may not be the best, but the opportunities for exerting influence and community leadership are great. A pulpit beats a soapbox for those motivated to persuade people to their own viewpoints.

There are other factors that play a role, and some are painful to relate. One ignoble motivation was felt sharply in the sixties. Seminary enrollment brought with it a deferment from the military draft. Some students were quite candid about it. A three-year tour of seminary seemed a better option than a tour of duty in Vietnam or exile to Canada.

But we dare not paint the whole house with the same

·brush. The vast majority of clergy are in the ministry out of a sincere desire to serve God. There are lots of sheep in sheep's clothing. Indeed, they are more than sheep; they are shepherds. These pastors love God and they love their people. With all their failings, they still try to please God and to lead other people to do so.

THE NEED FOR DOCTRINE

The church needs dedicated pastors. It also needs dedicated teachers of theology. The church has always benefited greatly from the work of sound theologians. I return again and again to the insights of Augustine, the cogency of Thomas Aquinas, the brilliance of Calvin, the passion of Luther. These men feed my mind and my soul.

We all need good teachers. I know that I cannot do without them. But how do we find them? What are the marks of a good teacher of theology?

Finding good teachers is like finding a good doctor. We want a doctor who knows what he is doing and who is a person we can trust with our bodies. If the doctor is warm and kind but doesn't know medicine, we are in deep trouble. It is small consolation to me if he holds my hand while he injects the wrong medicine into my bloodstream.

On the other hand, there are highly skilled professional physicians who have little personal regard for their patients. They know how to treat diseases but don't know how to treat people.

If possible, I want a doctor who is a master of medical knowledge and who will also value me as a person. Medically, that is the best of all possible worlds.

In theology we need teachers who display a high degree of skill and knowledge coupled with a deep love for God. Loving God is not a prejudicial barrier to a correct understanding of the things of God. On the contrary. A heart that is disposed toward God will only enhance the theologian's knowledge of God.

Professor G. C. Berkouwer of the Free University of Amsterdam once remarked in class, "Gentlemen, all great theologians begin and end their work with doxology!" Doxology—the writings of the great masters breathe a spirit of doxology. Their work goes beyond analysis and exposition to praise. Read the works of the apostle Paul, the premier theologian of the church. In the midst of his heaviest treatment of election he interrupts the flow of his thought to exclaim, "O the depths and the riches of His mercy!" (Romans 11:33).

We find that same spirit of doxology in the giants of church history. We can't miss it in Augustine, Athanasius, Anselm, Aquinas, Luther, Calvin, and Edwards, to mention the finest. None of these is infallible. We can find points of disagreement among them. Yet there is a remarkable and profound unity among them regarding the essential doctrines of the faith. Hear what C. S. Lewis once observed:

In the days when I still hated Christianity, I learned to recognize, like some all too familiar smell, that almost unvarying something which met me, now in Puritan Bunyan, now in Anglican Hooker, now in Thomist Dante. It was there (honeyed and floral) in Francois de

Sales; it was there (grave and homely) in Spenser and Walton; it was there (grim and manful) in Pascal and Johnson; there again, with a mild frightening, Paradisial flavor, in Vaughan and Boehme and Traherne. In the urban sobriety of the eighteenth century one was not safe—Law and Butler were two lions in the path. The supposed "Paganism" of the Elizabethans could not keep it out; it lay in wait where a man might have supposed himself safest, in the very centre of The Faerie Queene *and the* Arcadia. *It was, of course, varied; and yet—after all—so unmistakably the same; recognizable, not to be evaded, the odour which is death to us until we allow it to become life.* *

Now read the works of twentieth-century critical theologian Rudolf Bultmann. Bultmann displays an uncanny technical erudition. His critical skills are noteworthy. Yet it would require the lamp of Diogenes to find a single note of doxology in all his writings. That should tell us something. We do well to wonder if a man who cannot praise God is going to please God with his vast learning.

We still face the dilemma of a vast public fear of theology. At times I have been critical of Christian bookstores. So much of what sells as teaching is theologically weak. It is often not only simple (which is a virtue) but simplistic (which is a harmful vice). There is much doxology, but little theology. Some literature found in Christian bookstores manifests a serious ignorance of orthodox theology. It is simply bad teaching. It is well-intentioned bad teaching. But it is still bad teaching.

*C. S. Lewis, *God in the Dock*, ed. Walter Hooper (Grand Rapids: Eerdmans, 1970), 203-204.

For me to criticize Christian bookstores and Christian publishers is to bite the hand that feeds me. But if that hand is feeding harmful food to Christ's sheep then somebody needs to bite it.

I have pleaded with booksellers and publishers to promote the writings of the great masters. The usual response is that the great masters don't sell well to the general public. I still plead. I'm convinced that if the industry promoted the classics, the classics would sell.

I once ordered John Murray's *Principles of Conduct* for a seminary course. The publisher notified me that it was out of print. I pitched a fit. I begged the publisher to reprint it, even offering to raise the finances necessary to do it. The book was too important to allow it to slip into publishing purgatory. To my great joy the publisher relented and issued a new edition.

I would be delighted to see bookstores bury all my books in the basement or put them to the torch if they would replace them with the works of Luther, Augustine, Edwards, and the rest. What do I know that I haven't learned from them? The only difference between them and me is that their work is better thought out and much better written. I am sure that James Boice, J. I. Packer, Charles Colson, and a host of contemporary writers would say the same thing. We are at best dwarfs standing on the shoulders of the giants.

We need sound doctrine. The Spirit of holiness is also the Spirit of truth. Truth and righteousness go together. True living flows out of true thinking. Our lives can change externally without changing internally. All that achieves is to qualify us to be Pharisees. The Spirit goes to the root of the matter.

It is good trees that produce good fruit. It is the transformed mind that yields a transformed life. How we think about God is the most vital influence to how we respond to God. Repentance itself is a change of mind before it ever yields a change of behavior.

We must reject a false dichotomy between doctrine and life. We can have sound doctrine without a sanctified life. But it is extremely difficult to progress in sanctification without sound doctrine. Sound doctrine is not a sufficient condition to produce a sound life. It does not yield sanctification automatically. Sound doctrine is a *necessary* condition for sanctification. It is a vital prerequisite. It is like oxygen and fire. The mere presence of oxygen does not guarantee a fire, but you can't have a fire without it.

CONSCIOUSNESS, CONVICTION, CONSCIENCE

Why? Why is sound doctrine necessary for sanctification? For real sanctification to occur in the Christian life at least three absolute changes are necessary. There must be a change in our consciousness. There must be a change in our convictions. There must be a change in our conscience. Consciousness, conviction, and conscience—these three are all vital to our sanctification.

Consciousness involves knowledge. Before we can willfully do what God commands and what pleases Him, we must first understand what it is that God requires. From the Law comes a knowledge of sin. Also from the Law comes a knowledge of righteousness.

A person could "accidentally" obey the law without doing so consciously. But such an action would have no moral virtue to it. Suppose a man enjoys driving his car at fifty miles an hour. It pleases him to ride at that rate of speed. He drives his car at fifty miles an hour in fifty-five-mile-per-hour zones and in fifteen-mile-per-hour zones. When he drives in the fifty-five-mile-per-hour zone, he is within the speed limit. He is obeying the law. But when he goes fifty in a fifteen-mile-per-hour-zone, he is a menace to those around him.

Suppose our mythical driver systematically refuses to look at speed limit signs. He averts his gaze from any sign that even appears to mark a speed limit. He keeps himself purposefully unconscious of speed limits. At times he "happens" to obey the law, but purely by coincidence. If the man wants to achieve moral virtue as a driver and always drive within the speed limit, he must first become aware, he must become *conscious* of the law.

But consciousness is not enough. We all have seen people who are quite conscious of the speed limits while they are violating them. We don't have to look beyond ourselves to discover the culprits. For our behavior to change we must move beyond consciousness to conviction.

Conviction is a matter of depth and intensity. It is one thing to be aware that a certain action is right. It is another to have a conviction about it. It is a lot easier for us to compromise our knowledge than to act against convictions. A conviction is knowledge that is settled. It has a firm hold on us. It goes beyond our brains and penetrates the conscience.

Our conscience acts as a kind of governor upon our behavior. It is the inner voice that either accuses us or excuses us. It monitors our behavior by way of approval or disapproval. The problem is that our conscience doesn't always tell us the truth. We are adept at training it in the direction of self-approval.

It is hard to live with a guilty conscience. Guilt feelings paralyze us. They can produce literal nausea. They can provoke psychosomatic illnesses. When we are assaulted by a guilty conscience we can change our behavior or change our consciences. We can sear the conscience. We can dull its accusing tone by rationalization.

By repeating sins over and over again we can mute the inner voice of conscience. We fall into the decadence described by Paul in Romans 1 whereby we not only continue in sin but encourage others to join us in it.

Who, knowing the righteous judgment of God, that those who practice such things are worthy of death, not only do the same but also approve of those who practice them. Romans 1:32

Recently, I watched a segment of the Phil Donahue show that featured an interview of actors and actresses who starred in pornographic movies. The film players insisted that (a) they felt no guilt and (b) they had high standards because they refused to participate in radical sexual violence or in the sexual exploitation of children. They had a conscience about violence and child exploitation which "excused" their lack of conscience in other areas.

The porn actors justified their behavior by appealing to the fact that they avoided more heinous sexual behavior than their own. Their remarks were a consummate display of self-deceit, whereby they casually called evil good. They played on a distinction between bad and worse. They considered their own evil good because it was not worse. Here wickedness was relativized so that their own conscience could excuse them.

This game is played on more stages than those that are X-rated. As long as I can point to some worse evil than my own, I can flatter myself with a distorted view of virtue and vice.

For the conscience to function in a godly way it must be influenced by godly convictions. To gain godly consciences, our consciousness of what is right and what is wrong must be sharpened. This involves the mind. It is a matter of doctrine.

Doctrine comes from the Word of God. The Word addresses our consciousness. It is given for our understanding. The Word engages the mind, not the elbow. The Word is the Spirit's book. The Holy Spirit inspires the Scriptures. He is the Revealer of truth.

But the Spirit's work does not stop in the inspiring of Scripture. The Spirit illumines the Word and applies the Word to us:

But God has revealed them to us through His Spirit. For the Spirit searches all things, yes, the deep things of God. For what man knows the things of a man except

the spirit of the man which is in him? Even so no one
know the things of God except the Spirit of God.
1 Corinthians 2:10-11

I once heard Dr. David Hubbard, president of Fuller
Theological Seminary, speak on this text. Dr. Hubbard
explained the meaning of the Spirit's *searching* the things
of God. Human beings search after things they do not
have or do not know. The Holy Spirit is not an ignorant
member of the Godhead who is desperately seeking to
discover the truth of God. The Holy Spirit is God. All
that the Father knows the Spirit already knows—He does
not need to search after it.

Rather, the text refers to the Spirit's work of illumina-
tion for us. It is as though the Spirit puts a searchlight on
the Word of God to help us see what is already there. He
is assisting us in our search for understanding.

The Spirit is sent to instruct us and to convict us. He
applies the intensity of knowledge that is conviction. Jesus
promised the Holy Spirit for this purpose:

Nevertheless I tell you the truth. It is to your advantage
that I go away; for if I do not go away, the Helper will
not come to you; but if I depart, I will send Him to
you. And when He has come, He will convict the
world of sin, and of righteousness, and of judgment.
John 16:7-8

The progress from a changed consciousness to a
changed conviction to a changed conscience is directed by
the Holy Spirit. The Spirit works *with* the Word. He
does not work against the Word or without the Word.

The Word and Spirit go together. Doctrine and life go together. The will and the mind go together. To separate them is to frustrate the work of sanctification within us and to grieve the Holy Spirit. To separate them is to avoid the integrated, committed life that pleases God.

CHAPTER FIFTEEN

NEVER GIVE UP

ir Winston Churchill returned to Eton, the scene of his childhood education. The students were assembled to hear a speech from Eton's most illustrious alumnus. Churchill was a word merchant, a master of the English language without peer, the king of repartee. Of course, he had been challenged in debate on the floor of Parliament by unarmed men. Fools took him on at dinner parties, always to rue the moment. Even the great playwright George Bernard Shaw had mustered his wit to foil the prime minister. Shaw, on the occasion of the opening of one of his plays, dispatched an acid-dripping invitation to Churchill: "Dear Mr. Prime Minister, here are two complimentary tickets to the opening night of my new play. One ticket is for you and the other for a friend . . . if you have one."

Churchill dispatched an immediate reply: "Dear Mr. Shaw. Thank you for your invitation and generous gift of tickets for your new play. Unfortunately, my schedule prohibits my attending opening night. However, I shall surely be in attendance on the second night . . . if there is one."

By the time Churchill returned to Eton, his fame as a speaker was already well-known to every British schoolboy. The moment was at hand to hear the great man display his oratory. The assembly was hushed as Churchill approached the podium. He grasped the lectern and thrust out his chin in bulldog ferocity and said, "Never, never, never . . . give up." Then he sat down.

With one sentence he electrified his audience. One wonders how many times in how many young men's secret thoughts those words came back in a moment of crisis, a moment when the fearful totter between fight or flight.

Never give up. This is a message echoed again and again in Holy Writ. Consider Jesus the Author and the Finisher of our salvation. Jesus finishes what He starts. He did not spar with the Devil for a season. He locked the enemy in combat to the end.

One of the most significant utterances ever to come from the mouth of Jesus was spoken on the cross. In the midst of this grand passion, as He suffered the paroxysms of the agony of death, Jesus managed to gasp, "It is finished." That is when Jesus quit life. When His task was finished. Not before. Not until. The work had to be finished.

Jesus said, "No one, having put his hand to the plow, and looking back, is fit for the kingdom of God" (Luke 9:62). Jesus' eyes were fixed forward. He set his face toward Jerusalem. Lot's wife looked back and became a pillar of salt. Jesus looked ahead and achieved the redemption of the world.

Paul stated it this way: "Forgetting those things which are behind and reaching forward to those things which are ahead, I press toward the goal for the prize of the upward call of God in Christ Jesus" (Philippians 3:13-14).

We are called to *press* toward the mark of our high calling. To press is to use exertion. It is to apply pressure. The apostle is calling us to *effort*. The pursuit of righteousness is not a cavalier matter. There is no room for the easy-chair method of sanctification. Determination is important. Effort is important.

BOTH PASSIVE AND ACTIVE

One of the great distortions of the doctrine of sanctification may be found in the creed of quietism. Traditionally, quietism has referred to a kind of spiritual passivity that emphasizes divine activity and human inactivity. The popular slogan of quietism is, "Let go, and let God." The slogan has merit if it is intended to remind us that our spiritual progress cannot be achieved merely by our own efforts. Self-reformation is an exercise in futility if it proceeds without dependence upon the grace of God. But there is a better way to express this dependence. Rather than "Let go, and let God," we ought to say, "Hang on, and trust God."

To be sanctified involves work. The apostle exhorts Christians to a life of work:

Work out your own salvation with fear and trembling; for it is God who works in you both to will and to do for His good pleasure. Philippians 2:12-13

Sanctification is cooperative. There are two partners involved in the work. I must work and God will work. If ever the extra-biblical maxim, "God helps those who help themselves," had any truth, it is at this point. We are not called to sit back and let God do all the work. We are called to work, and to work hard. To work something out with fear and trembling is to work with devout and conscientious rigor. It is to work with care, with a profound concern with the end result.

I remember working in the yard as a boy. I worked on our family's yard as well as on the yards of our neighbors. I distinctly recall that I approached the tasks differently. When I worked at home my only concern was to finish the job in a hurry so I could go out and play. Trimming around trees and along sidewalks was either perfunctory or nonexistent.

Working in neighbors' yards was different. Here I was getting paid. My labor was being evaluated. I pressed harder. I paid more attention to detail. There was fear and trembling in my effort.

When I become a man I still had to do yard work. My care for detail went even deeper. Now I experienced *ownership*. It was *my* lawn I was working on. No one was paying me to trim around the trees. No one was looking over my shoulder to evaluate me. But it was *my* lawn. I wanted it to look nice. I cared about the results. (However, I was still in a hurry so I could go out and play!)

I was soon frustrated when I enlisted the help of my son. I noticed that he didn't care much about trimming around trees. He was fast with the mower. Zip, zip, the job was done. Not much fear. Not much trembling. He had a basketball game on the schedule. I thought to myself, *Doesn't he have any pride in our lawn?* Then I discovered the sins of the fathers being visited on the third generation. This wasn't a chip off the old block; this was the old block himself. I wonder if he will trim around trees when he has his own lawn. I suspect he will, for he, like everyone, will put forth effort when he sees the end result as important.

If we live to please God, we must constantly remind ourselves that our effort is extremely important. Our salvation doesn't end when we are reborn. True, the Spirit does the work of regeneration by Himself. Regeneration is monergestic, not synergistic. I am quiet, passive, when the Spirit does His work of quickening my soul. But then the work begins. I must work out my salvation. I must press toward the mark. Though the Spirit always helps us, we must *work* out our salvation.

THE VIOLENT PEOPLE OF THE KINGDOM

Jesus once made a remark that has puzzled Bible readers for centuries. He declared:

And from the days of John the Baptist until now the kingdom of heaven suffers violence, and the violent take it by force. Matthew 11:12

What did Jesus mean? How does the kingdom suffer violence? On the surface it seems to suggest that people can storm the gates of heaven and gain entrance by some sort of power play. It suggests that unworthy people can besiege the kingdom with military strength. But this interpretation does violence to everything the Bible teaches about the nature of God's kingdom. God is not powerless to prevent the unworthy from sneaking into His presence. No man by sheer effort can gain access to the Father.

God's fortress is not vulnerable to thieves and robbers. The pagan can lay siege to the heavenly Jerusalem yet never provoke the surrender of Zion.

No, I think Jonathan Edwards was correct when he saw this verse as referring to the passion by which new believers pursue their quest for God's kingdom. It describes the zeal by which those who are awakened by the Spirit press into the kingdom. With the announcement of John the Baptist of the approaching kingdom, a great awakening occurred in Israel. People flocked to the Jordan to receive the preparatory baptism of John.

Jesus took the announcement one step further. Where John said, "The kingdom of heaven is at hand" (Matthew 3:2), Jesus declared the very presence of the kingdom (Luke 17:21). With the appearance of Jesus the king of the kingdom arrived. This sparked an unprecedented national repentance. Those who were awakened *rushed* to embrace Christ. The repentant sinner leaves no stone unturned to embrace his king. The zeal and the passion of the newly awakened is forceful. It is violent not in the sense of the use of physical arms but in its urgency and intensity. (The New International Version reads "forceful men lay hold of it" instead of "the violent take it by force," and this may be a more accurate translation.)

This urgency and intensity requires a pressing into the kingdom. It means a determined effort with one's eyes fixed upon the goal. Indeed, there is an analogy drawn from warfare. When the gates of a walled city are opened, the victorious do not hesitate to push through. No soldier surrenders to lethargy or weariness at the moment of triumph.

Those who press into the kingdom sign up for the duration. We are not permitted the luxury of quitting. We cannot retire from sanctification. There are no pensions in the kingdom of God. We are called to endure to the end. When we dedicate ourselves to God, we dedicate ourselves to lifelong service. The phrase "full-time Christian service" applies not only to pastors and missionaries, but to everyone.

The author of the Epistle to the Hebrews describes the Christian life as a battle—even unto death.

Therefore we also, since we are surrounded by so great a cloud of witnesses, let us lay aside every weight, and the sin which so easily ensnares us, and let us run with endurance the race that is set before us, looking unto Jesus, the author and finisher of our faith. . . . You have not yet resisted to bloodshed, striving against sin.
Hebrews 12:1-2, 4

When we seek to overcome besetting sins we are easily frustrated, easily defeated. One straw breaks the back of the camel. We surrender before we resist unto blood.

Repeated failures do little to inspire confidence. This is why we are called to forget the things that are behind. We must forget the failures. We must not wallow in defeat. We must press on toward the mark. We must never, never, never give up.

Our goal is not trivial. It is worth fighting for. It is worth fear and trembling. It is the high calling of Christ.

Indeed, it is the highest calling. It is worth more effort than it takes to win a golf tournament. It is infinitely more important than trimming around trees. It is the calling of Jesus. It is worth all the blood, all the sweat, all the tears.

Again, the exhortation of the author of Hebrews is vivid:

Now no chastening seems to be joyful for the present, but grievous; nevertheless, afterward it yields the peaceable fruit of righteousness to those who have been trained by it. Therefore, strengthen the hands which hang down and the feeble knees, and make straight paths for your feet, so that what is lame may not be dislocated, but rather be healed. Hebrews 12:11-13

The author of Hebrews was elaborating on an earlier point.

And you have forgotten the exhortation which speaks to you as sons: "My son, do not despise the chastening of the Lord, nor be discouraged when you are rebuked by Him; for whom the Lord loves He chastens, and scourges every son whom He receives." Hebrews 12:5-6

Hebrews makes it clear that we are not bastards; we are sons. Our Father disciplines us precisely because He loves us. At times His hand is heavy upon us. That does not mean that He treats us in a heavy-handed manner. But the weight of His divine touch of discipline can easily overcome us. His chastening seems grievous. We respond with drooping hands and weak knees. Who wouldn't be weak-kneed in the face of divine discipline?

But the discipline of God is not meant to destroy us but

to heal us. The treatment is painful for a season. Knee braces are not comfortable. But the goal of the Father's discipline is training. It yields the fruit we are all seeking, the *peaceable fruit of righteousness.*

That fruit is worth the effort. It is worth the struggle. The discipline we endure is not worthy to be compared with the fruit that lies beyond it.

Here again are the words of Hebrews:

For you have not come to the mountain that may be touched and that burned with fire, and to blackness and darkness and tempest, and the sound of a trumpet and the voice of words, so that those who heard it begged that the word should not be spoken to them anymore. (For they could not endure what was commanded: "And if so much as a beast touches the mountain, it shall be stoned or thrust through with an arrow." And so terrifying was the sight that Moses said, "I am exceedingly afraid and trembling.") Hebrews 12:18-21

This is not our experience. Burning hills. Fierce storms. Black smoke. Sounds of trumpets and thundering words. This was the experience of the children of Israel at Mount Sinai. It was a time of terror. It left the people begging for relief. Even Moses was frightened in the extreme. The author mentions this ancient moment of terror for purposes of contrast:

But you have come to Mount Zion and to the city of the living God, the heavenly Jerusalem, to an innumerable company of angels, to the general assembly and church of the firstborn who are registered in heaven, to God the Judge of all, to the spirits of just men made perfect, to Jesus the Mediator of the new covenant, and to the blood of sprinkling that speaks better things than that of Abel. Hebrews 12:22-24

We are the new Israel. Our Exodus is infinitely greater than the one out of Egypt. Our Mediator dwarfs Moses by comparison. Our mountain is not Sinai but the eternal mountain of Zion. We enter into heaven. We join the multitude of angels. We enjoy the communion of all the saints. We are sprinkled by the blood of Christ, whose blood is of more import than all the sacrifices ever offered.

It is for this eternal home that we endure. Who can quit in such a venture? Who will not rise after stumbling to pursue afresh such a destiny?

There is a conclusion to the matter:

Therefore, since we are receiving a kingdom which cannot be shaken, let us have grace, by which we may serve God acceptably with reverence and godly fear. For our God is a consuming fire. Hebrews 12:28-29

It is for this consuming fire that we live. It is Him that we strive to please. It is for Him that we rise up again after repeated failures. It is He who is our destiny.